HR How-To: Employment Law

Everything you need to know to comply with the laws that govern every stage of the employment relationship ...

by Deborah Hammonds, J.D.
Kathleen B. Kapusta, J.D.

CCHKnowledgePoint®
Essential HR Solutions

A WoltersKluwer Company

Publisher: Catherine Wolfe
Editorial Director: Jeanne Statts
Portfolio Managing Editor: Mike Bacidore
Contributing Editors: Jan Gerstein, J.D.
                               Joy Waltemath, J.D.
Production Coordinator: Jennifer Lindt
Cover Design: Craig Arritola, Laila Gaidulis
Interior Design: Laila Gaidulis
Layout: Publications Design

This publication is designed to provide accurate and authoritative information in regard to the subject matter covered. It is sold with the understanding that the publisher is not engaged in rendering legal, accounting, or other professional service. If legal advice or other expert assistance is required, the services of a competent professional person should be sought.

ISBN 0-8080-1006-9
©2003 **CCH** Incorporated
4025 W. Peterson Ave.
Chicago, IL 60646-6085
1 800 248 3248
hr.cch.com

A WoltersKluwer Company

All Rights Reserved
Printed in the United States of America

Acknowledgements

We would like to express our thanks and appreciation to all the people who have helped to make this book possible. It truly has been a pleasure working with all of you. To Joy Waltemath and Jan Gerstein, thank you for your support, guidance, encouragement and editorial expertise throughout this entire process.

To Laila Gaidulis, thank you for your ability to turn our vague ideas into creative and unique cartoon illustrations that really bring these pages to life. To Craig Arritola, thank you for your production assistance and dynamic cover design. To Jennifer Lindt, thank you also for your production assistance, the hours spent reviewing our words, and your wonderful attention to detail. To Cynthia Hackerott, thank you for your work on indexing this book.

Special thanks to Marjorie Johnson for helping with the day-to-day workload and also to Joyce Gentry, Cynthia Hackerott, and Robyn McCain for not only taking on extra work to make writing this book possible but also for your constant support, advice and encouragement.

And last but not least, we would like to thank our families for their never-ending support and encouragement.

Deborah Hammonds
Kathleen B. Kapusta
August 2003

Contents

Chapter 1	Introduction to employment law	1
Chapter 2	Choosing your work force	15
Chapter 3	Compensation practices	43
Chapter 4	Performance appraisals	81
Chapter 5	Time away from work	103
Chapter 6	Discrimination	129
Chapter 7	Harassment	153
Chapter 8	Discipline	169
Chapter 9	Employee relations	195
Chapter 10	Termination	215

Chapter

1

Introduction to employment law

High cost of employee lawsuits 2
Key federal employment laws 2
State law as source of employee rights 8
Employment law violations: Know the consequences 9
    BEST PRACTICES: Take these actions
        to avoid legal trouble 12
The Quiz 13

> *Yolanda, a part-time sales associate who has been working for your department store for several years, takes medication in an attempt to control her epilepsy. Yolanda's seizures, although sporadic, occur frequently enough that she is prohibited from driving. Your organization has allowed her to take several medical leaves because of her condition. Despite her condition, Yolanda has worked successfully in various departments in your store.*
>
> *After her most recent leave, Yolanda was released to return to work with one restriction–that she not climb a ladder until she has been free of seizures for six months (she was most recently assigned to the shoe department, where ladder-climbing to check stock is required). Your organization tells her that she cannot return to work if she is under any medical restrictions, and when she inquires about the availability of a position in another department (where ladder-climbing isn't required), she again is told she cannot return with a medical restriction.*
>
> *Yolanda is terminated and sues for disability discrimination. Shortly after Yolanda's termination, your organization hires two new sales associates in departments that do not require ladder climbing.*

> *Your company doesn't believe that Yolanda is disabled as a matter of law because you know that under recent Supreme Court decisions, disability status is determined on an individual basis and takes into account corrective measures, including medication, taken to mitigate any disability. You don't believe that a ladder-climbing restriction substantially limits a major life activity as required by law. Are you successful in defending the lawsuit?*

High cost of employee lawsuits

Worried that your front line managers don't understand the importance of preventing workplace discrimination? You should be. While the results of one national survey suggest that employee lawsuits are declining, if your organization is sued for employment law violations, the costs can be staggering.

According to one study, the average jury award for wrongful termination is about $400,000. Some companies have even been slapped with multimillion dollar verdicts. And if a company enters a settlement to stop employment litigation, it still may shell out a hefty sum. Settlements have been as high as $250,000,000. That should get your managers' and supervisors' attention.

Key federal employment laws

Many of the key federal employment laws protect employees from discrimination in employment. These discrimination laws are designed to require that all persons be given equal opportunity in employment. Various laws are directed toward the protection of individuals in their civil right to take, hold and advance in a job free of discrimination based on specified personal characteristics.

Employment discrimination laws touch all phases of the employment experience, including:
- compensation and fringe benefits;
- discipline;
- employment referrals;
- hiring decisions;
- job assignments;
- layoffs and downsizing;

Chapter 1—Introduction to employment law

- promotions;
- recruiting;
- screening of applicants;
- training;
- union representation;
- work rules;
- working atmosphere.

When discrimination occurs, employers have an affirmative duty to take the necessary measures to eliminate the effects of the discriminatory acts or practices.

DON'T miss this

What do I need to know to comply? Following is a quick rundown on what you need to know to comply with the major employment laws.

Title VII of the Civil Rights Act of 1964

Employer coverage: Generally both private and public employers.

Number of employees: 15 or more.

Requirements of law: Bans discrimination in all areas of the employer-employee relationship—from advertisements for help through termination or retirement—on the basis of race, color, sex, religion, or national origin.

What if there was no intent to discriminate?

You don't have to purposefully discriminate to get into legal trouble.

WHAT you need to know

When an employment practice or policy that on its face looks nondiscriminatory has a disproportionately discriminatory impact on minorities, it is called "disparate" or "adverse impact" discrimination. No motive is required for disparate impact discrimination. Employers need to guard against the possibility that their actions might result in disparate impact discrimination, which is also prohibited under federal law.

Administering agency: Equal Employment Opportunity Commission.

Americans with Disabilities Act of 1990

Employer coverage: Generally both private and public employers.

Number of employees: 15 or more.

Requirements of law: Requires a covered employer to make reasonable accommodations to the known physical or mental limitations of an otherwise qualified job applicant or employee with a disability, unless it can be demonstrated that the required accommodation would impose an undue hardship on the operation of the employer's business.

> In general, an accommodation is any change in the work environment or in the way things are customarily done that enables an individual with a disability to enjoy equal employment opportunities. There are three categories of reasonable accommodation. These are:
> - accommodations that are required to ensure equal opportunity in the application process;
> - accommodations that enable employees with disabilities to perform the essential functions of the position held or desired; and
> - accommodations that enable employees with disabilities to enjoy the same benefits and privileges of employment as are enjoyed by employees without disabilities.

Administering agency: Equal Employment Opportunity Commission.

Age Discrimination in Employment Act of 1967

Employer coverage: Generally both private and public employers.

Number of employees: 20 or more.

Requirements of law: Prohibits discrimination against persons who are at least 40 years of age, but allows mandatory retirement of highly compensated executives or top policy makers who have

Chapter 1—Introduction to employment law

reached 65 years of age and who stand to receive at least $44,000 annually in pension payments.

> An ammendment to the law provides that although an employer must provide equal benefits to all employees, if the cost of providing a benefit to an older employee is greater than providing the same benefit to a younger worker, the employer can provide smaller benefits to the older worker—as long as the employer spends the same amount for all employees.

Administering agency: Equal Employment Opportunity Commission.

Equal Pay Act of 1963

Employer coverage: Generally both private and public employers.

Number of employees: No minimum.

Requirements of law: Prohibits the payment of workers of one sex at a rate different from that paid the other sex for substantially equal work in the same establishment.

> *Differences in pay are not unlawful if they result from a seniority system, a merit system, a system that measures earnings by the quantity or quality of production, or by any factor other than sex.*

Administering agency: Equal Employment Opportunity Commission.

Uniformed Services Employment and Reemployment Rights Act of 1994

Employer coverage: All civilian employers.

Number of employees: No minimum.

Requirements of law: Prohibits employment discrimination because of past, current, or future military obligations. Provides military leave and reemployment rights.

Is the ban on discrimination separate from any right of reemployment eligibility? The protection from discrimination is completely separate from the right to reemployment for eligible persons following military service.

Consequently, reemployment eligibility is not a prerequisite to discrimination protection.

What if an employer has other reasons for its action? When a *motivating factor* for an employer's adverse employment action is an individual's past, present or future connection with service, the employer can avoid liability only by proving that it would have taken the same action regardless of the individual's connection with the service.

*Liability is possible when service connection is **just one** of several reasons for the action. To avoid liability, the employer must prove that a reason **other than** service connection would have been sufficient to justify its action.*

Administering agency: Veterans Employment and Training Service, Department of Labor.

Immigration Reform and Control Act of 1986

Employer coverage: All employers.

Number of employees: Hiring of unauthorized workers: No minimum. National origin discrimination: 4 to 14. *Citizenship discrimination:* 4 or more.

Requirements of law: Bans the hiring of unauthorized workers. Requires verification of employment eligibility on Form I-9 and prohibits documentation discrimination. Bans discrimination in hiring or discharge on the basis of national origin and citizenship status.

Chapter 1—Introduction to employment law

> Employers may give preference to a citizen over a noncitizen if the two candidates are equally qualified.

Administering agency: Bureau of Immigration and Customs Enforcement, Department of Justice and the Department of Labor's Office of Federal Contract Compliance Programs (eligibility verification); Office of the Special Counsel, Department of Justice (discrimination).

Family and Medical Leave Act of 1990

Employer coverage: Private and public employers.

Number of employees: Private employers must employ 50 or more.

Requirements of law: Guarantees an employee up to 12 weeks of job-protected, unpaid leave each year for any one or more of the following reasons:
- the birth or adoption of a child;
- the serious health condition of a child, spouse, or parent;
- the employee's own serious illness or pregnancy.

> FMLA leave is unpaid although employers can require employees to take paid leave they have already earned (such as vacation or sick leave) during FMLA leave.

Administering agency: Department of Labor.

National Labor Relations Act

Employer coverage: Private employers involved in interstate commerce.

Number of employees: No minimum.

Requirements of law: Gives employees the right to unionize, the right to bargain collectively, and the right to engage in other activities for their mutual aid and protection.

WHAT you need to know: Employees do not have to belong to a union to be protected by the NLRA.

Administering agency: National Labor Relations Board.

State law as source of employee rights

Most states have employment laws that provide the same rights as those provided under the federal employment laws. Some state employment laws grant even greater rights, however. For instance, discrimination on the basis of sexual orientation, political affiliation, marital status, nursing mother status, genetic information, or off-duty conduct may be prohibited under state law.

Law created by the courts is yet another source of employee rights. Below are some state court theories under which an employee may sue an employer:

- ◆ **Infliction of emotional distress:** The employee suffered severe emotional distress as a result of abusive treatment in the workplace.
- ◆ **Defamation:** A false or malicious statement (either written or spoken) was made about the employee that resulted in damage to the employee's reputation.
- ◆ **Invasion of privacy:** A supervisor publicly disclosed private facts about the employee, such as the details of a performance appraisal.
- ◆ **Interference with employment:** A supervisor tried to get the employee fired, or to botch his or her chances of getting or keeping a new job, in order to gain personal revenge or advantage.
- ◆ **Fraud or negligent misrepresentation:** The employee suffered harm as a result of reliance on false statements made to the employee about job security, performance evaluations, health hazards, or some other employment matter.
- ◆ **Negligent employment:** The employee was injured by a co-worker whom the company knew or should have known could harm others.

- **False imprisonment:** The employee was detained or restrained against the employee's will.
- **Battery:** The employee was subjected to harmful or offensive conduct.
- **Assault:** The employee was threatened with harmful or offensive contact.
- **Constructive discharge:** The employee resigned in response to working conditions that the employee found intolerable.
- **Discharge in violation of public policy:** The employee was fired for exercising a legal right, such as filing a workers' compensation claim; satisfying a legal obligation, serving on a jury or making a required court appearance; or reporting or protesting the organization's illegal conduct.
- **Breach of contract:** An explicit written or spoken employment-related promise (such as a formal agreement to employ the employee for a set number of years) was broken.
- **Breach of implied contract:** An implicit employment-related promise (such as a supervisor's comments implying job security for the employee, or a personnel handbook statement implying that specific disciplinary procedures will be followed before anyone is fired) was broken.

Employment law violations: Know the consequences

Remedies that courts may order for violations of employment rights include:
- Rehiring of someone who was illegally fired.
- Hiring of an applicant who was illegally refused employment.
- Back pay (paying wages to an illegally fired employee for the period he or she was out of work).
- Double back pay for willful violations of certain laws.
- Front pay (payment of future wages that would have been earned if an employee had not been illegally fired).
- Compensatory damages for losses suffered as a result of illegal conduct.

- Losses that a company may be ordered to pay for include:
  - Nonmonetary losses (emotional pain, suffering, inconvenience, mental anguish, loss of enjoyment of life);
  - Future monetary losses (expected losses due to inability to work, future medical expenses); and
  - Past monetary losses (doctor's bills, money spent in seeking another job).
- Punitive damages to punish severe violations.
- Payment of an employee's attorney and expert witness fees.

Additional consequences

Violations of the employment laws can also result in:
- Lost productive time of persons involved in resolving claims of unlawful conduct.
- Low employee morale.
- High employee turnover.
- Harm to the company's reputation and business.
- Government involvement in the company's business practices.

Let's take another look at Yolanda's termination. Will your organization be successful in defending her lawsuit? Probably not. Individuals who take medicine to lessen the symptoms of an impairment so that they can function may still be substantially limited in a major life activity and, therefore, be disabled under the Americans with Disabilities Act. Yolanda's medical restriction revealed that despite medication, her seizures were not under control at the time of her termination.

The case goes to trial and your organization argues that when it decided to discharge Yolanda, she was not, as medicated, substantially limited in a major life activity as required by the Americans with Disabilities Act because the only work

> *activity she was prohibited from performing was ladder-climbing. While ladder-climbing is not a major life activity, the court learns that during her seizures Yolanda could not speak, walk, see, work, or control the left side of her body. In determining Yolanda's status under the ADA, the court decides that these are major life activities.*
>
> *Moreover, the court decides that there is sufficient evidence that your organization acted with malice or reckless indifference to Yolanda's federally protected rights under the ADA and awards punitive damages. Your organization's policy was not to allow employees with any restrictions to return to work. No exceptions are made to accommodate disabilities. And, although Yolanda's manager was aware that federal law imposed a duty to attempt to accommodate the restrictions of disabled individuals, he made no effort whatsoever to explore any possibility that would allow Yolanda to return to work with her ladder-climbing restriction. Yet shortly after her termination the company hired two new sales associates in departments that did not require ladder climbing.*

The decision to terminate Yolanda could indeed cost your organization in a number of ways. Punitive damages and court costs are the most obvious. But there are also the indirect costs that are not so readily assigned a dollar figure—for example, court or agency interference in the structuring of business practices, and the loss of productivity on the part of all involved in the resolution of the case.

What steps can you take to avoid lawsuits and reduce the risks of liability if your organization is sued?

Best Practices

Take these actions to avoid legal trouble

Actions you can take and teach your managers and supervisors to take to prevent lawsuits and reduce the risk of liability if your organization is sued include:

- Learn what the employment laws are and what rights and protections employees have under them.
- Use only job-related factors as the basis for employment decisions.
- Apply work rules in the same way to all employees.
- Treat people as individuals and in a respectful manner that recognizes the valuable contribution each person makes to the company.
- Use performance appraisals and discipline not as punishment, but as positive tools for improving employee job performance or conduct.
- Give employees honest, accurate feedback.
- Never discipline or fire someone without first checking out whether doing so is fair, legal, and consistent with company policies.
- Document employees' performance.
- Watch what you say.
    - Don't make rude or discriminatory remarks.
    - Don't make employment promises.
    - Don't interpret benefit plans.
    - Don't make false or mean comments about employees.
    - Don't discuss disciplinary issues concerning an employee except with persons who have a legitimate right to know.
    - Don't broadcast private facts about an employee.
    - Don't respond to a reference check without first checking company policy.
    - Don't threaten employees who engage in union activity.
- Take seriously employees' complaints about harassment, misconduct, wages, hours, job conditions, injuries, and company practices that may harm the public or violate the law.

These actions are not just useful in avoiding lawsuits. They also serve as basic steps to good personnel management. Management of people in general, including the process of discipline, should be viewed as a way to build a work force of productive persons. Take these steps first to educate your managers and supervisors and second to keep your company out of legal trouble.

The Quiz

1. When discrimination occurs, employers have an affirmative duty to take the necessary measures to eliminate the effects of the discriminatory acts or practices. ❑ True ❑ False

2. State employment laws can never grant greater rights than federal employment laws. ❑ True ❑ False

3. Violations of employment can result in (choose one):
   a. low employee morale
   b. high employee turnover
   c. harm to the company's reputation
   d. government involvement in the organization's business practices
   e. all of the above
   f. none of the above

4. Employment decisions should be based on job-related factors only. ❑ True ❑ False

5. Unintentional discrimination isn't unlawful. ❑ True ❑ False

Answer key: 1. T; 2. F; 3. e; 4. T; 5. F

Chapter 2

Choosing your work force

Hiring concerns: Staying out of court 16
Avoiding discrimination claims: EEO compliance 17
Job descriptions: Defining your hiring needs 19
    BEST PRACTICES: Use job description
        to make more informed hiring decisions 21
ADA and reasonable accommodation 22
Recruitment practices 24
    BEST PRACTICES: Phrases to avoid in employment ads 25
Interviewing: If you don't need to know, don't ask 26
Avoid making promises 29
Pre-employment testing 29
    BEST PRACTICES: Pre-employment testing guidelines 31
Reference and background checks 32
The job offer 37
Immigration recordkeeping requirements 39
    BEST PRACTICES: Complying with immigration law
        requirements 40
Document your decision 41
The Quiz 42

Tim, a manager in your organization, has been interviewing applicants for a secretarial position. The classified ad has been running for ten days, but only two candidates have applied. The first candidate, Alethea, an African American woman, arrived for her interview dressed in jeans with holes in them, a tee shirt, and scuffed tennis shoes. Rather than noting what Alethea was wearing, Tim simply wrote "wrong appearance" on her application.

*   Rosa, the second candidate, has extensive experience, but she has not remained in any one position for more than two years. Although her residence remains the same, Rosa takes*

positions that are located in different areas of town, even when that causes a substantial commute. She has repeated that pattern in three cities.

You know there are problems with both candidates but you're getting pressure to fill that position quickly. What should you do? How do you avoid making the wrong decision?

Hiring concerns: Staying out of court

Hiring decisions have a profound impact on your organization, from both a general business and a legal standpoint. Hiring decisions can do enormous good or subject the organization to legal liability.

Inappropriate questions asked during an interview, the wrong comments penciled as notes, or even a promise made in haste to an applicant, could land your organization in court.

As you proceed through the hiring process—from recruitment to the job offer—there are three main legal areas to be concerned about: unlawful discrimination; negligent hiring; and the making and breaking of promises.

Unlawful discrimination. Most employers are covered by Title VII of the 1964 Civil Rights Act, which prohibits employment discrimination on the basis of race, sex, religion, color and national origin. The Americans with Disabilities Act (ADA) prohibits employment discrimination based on disability. Age bias is also outlawed. Discrimination against members of a labor organization is prohibited, as is discrimination based on military status. The Immigration Reform and Control Act of 1986 bans discrimination on the basis of citizenship, although employers may give preference to a citizen over an equally qualified alien. State laws may add arrest record, marital status, sexual orientation and other categories.

> Claims of discrimination arise when employers make, or appear to make, employment decisions based on these protected characteristics; characteristics that have nothing to do with a person's ability to do the job.

Negligent hiring. Generally, employers always have been held responsible for the behavior of their employees while performing their jobs. Negligent hiring is a concept that goes much further–the employer is responsible when the employee, acting outside the scope of his or her job, commits an act that injures someone else–another employee, a customer, or an innocent bystander. Under a claim of "negligent hiring," the person who was injured contends that it was the negligence of the employer that put the employee in a position where the employee could hurt someone. The employer failed to uncover the employee's incompetence or unfitness by checking references, criminal records or general background information.

Making or breaking of contracts. Making or breaking of contracts occurs most often by promising an applicant something you may or may not be able to deliver, like saying, "You'll have a job for life," or "You can't be discharged without just cause." Employee handbooks may contain language that might be interpreted by a court as promising job security.

> *Progressive discipline policies and probationary periods for new employees, for example, can form the basis for an "implied" employment contract.*

Avoiding discrimination claims: EEO compliance

Equal employment opportunity compliance is one of the most important legal considerations at the hiring stage. How can you ensure that hiring decisions are free of bias? Two key questions are important in making that determination.

Does the decision-maker understand the job? Individuals in charge of interviewing and hiring commit the organization by their statements and actions. Therefore, it is very important that they understand what they are doing:
- ◆ Do persons within the organization who make hiring decisions know the essential functions that must be performed in each job for which they hire?
- ◆ Do they know the qualifications that a person must meet to perform those jobs?
- ◆ Are interviewers provided with job descriptions and job specifications?

How was the decision made?
- ◆ Throughout the hiring process, are decisions based on job requirements, not on extraneous factors that may be viewed as discriminatory?
- ◆ Do the qualifications and requirements of a job arise out of the job itself and are they free of discriminatory impact?
- ◆ Is the ability of an applicant to perform a job *the* criteria to support a hiring decision?

Remember Tim, the manager who wrote "wrong appearance" on Alethea's application after interviewing her? Although Tim was referring to the holes in Alethea's jeans and her scuffed tennis shoes, it might be difficult to convince a jury that his hastily scribbled note wasn't a reference to the fact that Alethea is African American. Tim's comment could easily be viewed as discriminatory. Tim should review the qualifications for the job and make sure that all questions and comments-even notes penciled on an application-relate to those requirements.

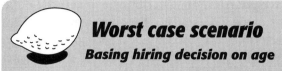

Worst case scenario
Basing hiring decision on age

A 63-year-old man with 38 years of experience as a clinical dentist applied for an "entry-level" position with a public agency. The agency rejected the dentist in favor of younger candidates with much less experience. A federal court determined that the agency engaged in unlawful age discrimination when it refused to hire the dentist. The court said it was inappropriate for the agency to reject the applicant in favor of dentists with only three or four years of experience because he did not conform to the stereotype for an entry-level job. The agency's stated reasons for rejecting the dentist—he was "over-qualified" for the position, there was a short gap in his experience, and there were questions about his ability to work with adults and the low income, city populace—were excuses for discriminatory selection. The gap, noted the court, did not affect the applicant's ability. Moreover, he previously handled adult problems, and worked at a hospital serving low income and inner city inhabitants.

Solution: Make sure you don't rely unwittingly on stereotypes; instead base your decision on the applicant's ability to perform the job.

Job descriptions: Defining your hiring needs

There is no specific legal requirement that an employer have written job descriptions, but there are some very good reasons to have them. In order to identify and hire qualified candidates, a clear understanding of the job and its necessary qualifications is required. An up-to-date job description is an excellent source for this information.

Think of a job description as a road map for finding and hiring the right person for the position.

What is a job description? A job description explains the duties and responsibilities of the job itself, not the characteristics of specific individuals performing the job. Therefore, one job description typically applies to numerous employees.

> Avoid even the mention of impermissible factors such as race, religion, national origin, age, sex or disability in a job description. These carry a presumption of not being job-related.

Job descriptions also contain job specifications, which describe the minimum level of knowledge, skills and abilities that employees need to perform the job's essential functions. Examples of job specifications include level of education, type of experience, and mental and physical abilities.

> *Hiring decisions should not be based on knowledge, skills and abilities that are not listed in the job description. If these qualifications are truly needed to perform the essential functions of the job, make sure they are included in the description.*

Defining essential functions

Job descriptions should ideally distinguish between essential and non-essential job functions. Essential functions are the fundamental duties that describe why a job exists, while non-essential functions describe desirable, but not critical, aspects of a job.

> **Example:** *Driving a bus and obeying all traffic laws are essential functions of a bus driver job because they define why the position exists. Incidental activities performed by a bus driver, such as searching for lost items or picking up litter, are most likely nonessential functions of the job.*

Chapter 2—Choosing your work force 21

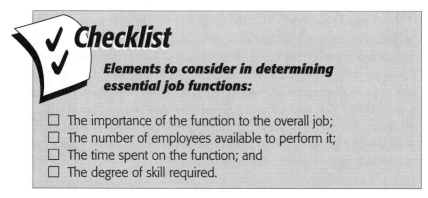

Checklist

Elements to consider in determining essential job functions:

- ☐ The importance of the function to the overall job;
- ☐ The number of employees available to perform it;
- ☐ The time spent on the function; and
- ☐ The degree of skill required.

Be careful about the qualification requirements that are established for particular jobs. If job qualifications are set unreasonably high, they may have the discriminatory effect of screening out greater proportions of legally protected groups. For this reason, job qualifications should not be thought of as wish lists. They need to be stated in terms of realistic minimum requirements that are necessary to perform the job competently.

Best Practices

Use job description to make more informed hiring decisions

By reviewing the current job description for a position vacancy, a manager can direct the job search toward a person with the exact competencies the job requires.

Because required qualifications are clearly spelled out on paper and duties are carefully delineated, managers are better able to ask questions as they conduct interviews.

A detailed list of the competencies a job requires helps keep a manager on track. The job description provides an objective basis for comparison of each candidate's qualifications with the requirements of the job.

A written job description also represents the conditions management and workers agree to at the beginning of their employer/employee relationship.

ADA and reasonable accommodation

Focusing on the job's essential functions and the qualifications that are necessary to perform those functions is also important for purposes of complying with the ADA. The ADA requires covered employers to make reasonable accommodations to the known physical or mental limitations of an otherwise qualified job applicant with a disability, unless the employer can demonstrate that the required accommodation would impose an undue hardship on the operation of its business.

DON'T miss this

Denying employment opportunities to an applicant who is a qualified individual with a disability is discrimination if the decision is based on the individual's need for reasonable accommodation.

Under the ADA, a person has a disability if he or she has a physical or mental impairment that substantially limits a major life activity such as hearing, seeing, speaking, breathing, performing manual tasks, walking, caring for oneself, learning or working. The ADA also protects individuals who have a record of a substantially limiting impairment, and people who are regarded as having a substantially limiting impairment.

Being qualified to perform the essential functions of the job means that the applicant must:

- satisfy the job requirements for educational background, employment experience, skills, licenses, and any other qualification standards that are job related; and
- be able to perform those tasks that are essential to the job, with or without reasonable accommodation.

A reasonable accommodation is a modification or adjustment that would enable the person to perform the job functions. A reasonable accommodation should be tailored to the needs of the individual and the requirements of the job.

✓ Checklist

Selecting employees and complying with the ADA

- [ ] You must consider hiring a qualified disabled applicant if he or she can perform the job with "reasonable accommodation," but only if you will not incur undue hardship.
- [ ] You are free to select the most qualified applicant available and to make decisions based on reasons unrelated to the existence or consequence of a disability.
- [ ] You are not required to lower quality or quantity standards to make an accommodation, nor are you obligated to provide personal use items such as glasses or hearing aids.
- [ ] Retraining or placing disabled employees in jobs that require no accommodation is sometimes an available alternative.
- [ ] You can refuse to hire an applicant or fire a current employee who is illegally using drugs.
- [ ] Testing for the use of illegal drugs is permissible under the ADA.
- [ ] Legislative history indicates that Congress intended the ADA to protect persons with AIDS and HIV-related diseases from discrimination.
- [ ] Review your job descriptions to make certain that they establish the job requirements so far as reasonably possible; too broad a description might enable a disabled person to qualify for a job that he or she could not actually perform.
- [ ] Omit all references in advertisements for jobs and job descriptions to nonessential or marginal requirements.
- [ ] Carefully document what was done or could be done to accommodate an employee or applicant.
- [ ] Review and revise all employment application forms and other hiring and employment materials, including materials for staff use, and delete all references to an applicant's medical history and physical appearance.
- [ ] Visual impressions of an applicant's disability should not be used in any way to discriminate, such as recording them on a file jacket or using a secret code.
- [ ] Both the employee with a disability and the company will benefit if the manager focuses on the person's abilities rather than his or her disability.

Recruitment practices

Does your organization tend to attract younger workers over older workers, or one gender, ethnic group, or racial group to the exclusion of others? The EEOC warns that the following methods may raise EEOC compliance concerns.

Potential discrimination concerns in recruiting

- **Walk-ins.** Advertising job openings and accepting applications only at your place of business could be discriminatory because it depends entirely on your location and workforce. If your location is in an all-white or predominately white neighborhood, non-whites may be deterred from applying. If you are a restaurant or retail store catering to the young, older people may be deterred. If your workforce is almost entirely white, female or young, then walk-ins might be deterred from applying, because they believe that they will not be hired if they are not white, female or young.
- **Word-of-mouth referrals.** This approach could also be discriminatory depending on your workforce. For example, if your workforce is almost entirely white, male or young, then word-of-mouth referrals may reinforce the non-diverse nature of the workforce and may be found by some courts to discriminate against persons who are not white, male or young.
- **Online recruiting and resume scanning.** While the new technologies make it easier for employers to locate job seekers and process the thousands of resumes received each year, they have also raised unanswered EEO concerns in the area of applicant-flow data and defining the applicant pool. Must you track every resume received from online applicants for EEO purposes? It's still an open question.
- **Referral fees and bonuses.** Offering finder's fees to employees who refer another person for employment can cause the same problems as word-of-mouth referrals if your workforce is non-diverse.

- ◆ **Employment agencies.** Relying on employment agencies to screen employees can cause problems if you do not make it clear that agencies should observe equal employment opportunity laws.
- ◆ **Hiring halls/union membership.** Another form of discrimination that is outlawed by the federal government is bias based on a job applicant's union membership or lack of it. Employers who use union hiring halls for employee referrals must be careful to avoid granting favorable status to union members.

Focusing on the job description rather than extraneous factors throughout the entire hiring process can help avoid even unintended references to protected characteristics.

 Best Practices

Phrases to avoid in employment ads

The EEOC recommends avoiding the following phrases.
- ◆ "Recent college graduate" (potential Age Discrimination in Employment Act violation)
- ◆ "0-1 years of experience" (potential Age Discrimination in Employment Act violation)
- ◆ "Young, energetic" (potential Age Discrimination in Employment Act violation)
- ◆ "Hostess" or "waitress" (potential sex discrimination in violation of Title VII)
- ◆ "Christian carpenter wanted" (potential religious discrimination in violation of Title VII)

Interviewing: If you don't need to know, don't ask

Federal law does not expressly prohibit pre-employment inquiries concerning a job applicant's race, religion, sex, national origin or age. But that does not make them appropriate either. State laws may explicitly prohibit some of these questions. And the mere fact that a question was asked can be used in a trial as evidence of discrimination.

In choosing interview questions, consider:
1. Will the answer to this question, if used in making a selection, have the effect of screening out members of a protected group?
2. Is this information really needed to judge an applicant's competence or qualifications for the job in question?

WHAT you need to know

The job description can serve as a basis for preparing a written interview guide. Following a written guide helps to ensure consistency, minimizes the risk of asking improper questions and assists in documenting the interview process.

Avoid questions that are not demonstrably related to the job

Avoid questions about a person's race, color, sex, religion, national origin, age, disability or anything that could be construed as asking about those factors unless it is demonstrably necessary to make a hiring decision for the job in question. For example, there may be a minimum age requirement for a particular job, in which case it is appropriate to ask: "Are you of legal age to work?"

Avoid questions that appear to be job-related but are asked only of certain candidates. For example, female candidates for a flight attendant position should not be asked if they are married, whether they have children, and, if so, whether they are too attached to their children to be away from them for long periods of time. Instead, all candidates for the position may be asked: "Is there anything that would prevent you from being able to endure unexpected layovers?"

Avoid questions that are "neutral" but have been shown to have an adverse or negative impact on certain groups, or present a risk of doing so. For example, questions about height and weight should be avoided unless these standards are absolutely essential to the safe performance of the job and there are no alternatives to the standard.

Other potential problem areas include:

Marital or family status. Asking about marital status or children is not job-related and may be impermissible under state law.

Citizenship. An inquiry into an applicant's citizenship may be evidence of discrimination on the basis of national origin. Both citizens and non-citizens are afforded protection against national origin bias. You may legally ask whether an applicant is authorized to work in the U.S. See Immigration recordkeeping requirements, below.

Residence. Don't ask about an applicant's ownership or rental of a residence or length at an address. However, it is appropriate to ask an applicant where he or she can be reached.

Crimes. Asking whether an applicant has been arrested or charged with a crime may be impermissible in some states. Arrest alone does not mean the person committed the crime charged. Using arrest information to screen applicants can also have an adverse impact on minority applicants and, therefore, should normally not be asked. Asking about convictions is different, but employers should consider the nature of the offense in relation to the job requirements as well as time elapsed since the conviction and evidence of rehabilitation. It's probably better to conduct criminal reference checking outside the initial interview. However, if there are any gaps in an applicant's employment record, the applicant can be asked why he or she was not working during those times

Health or disabilities. The ADA and many state laws impose an outright ban on asking disability-related questions before a job offer is made.

A disability-related question is any question that is likely to elicit information about a disability.

This includes questions such as: "Do you have any physical or mental disabilities that will keep you from performing this job?"; "Do you have a drug or alcohol problem?"; or "Have you ever received workers' compensation benefits?" This also includes asking questions that solicit information suggesting the presence or non-presence of a disability, such as asking if the applicant takes prescription drugs, or how many days he or she missed from work in the past year due to an illness. But you can explain the job functions and ask how the applicant would perform the job, as long as all applicants for the job are asked this.

> Once a conditional job offer is made to an applicant, the applicant can be asked disability-related questions as long as all entering employees in the same job category are asked the same questions.

Current or future military service. Applicants should not be asked about any military obligations or whether they expect to serve in the military.

Veteran status or military discharge. Questions such as "Are you a veteran?" or "Were you ever in the military?" are inappropriate. But applicants can be asked: "Do you have any special skills, experience, or training that would qualify you for this job?" Other questions to avoid include: "What kind of military discharge did you receive?" or "Were you ever disciplined in the military?"

Education. Asking whether an applicant has a high school or other specific educational degree is inappropriate unless the degree is a job-related requirement.

Religion. An inquiry into an applicant's religion is not job-related unless your organization is a religious institution entitled to give preference to applicants of the same religion. Additionally, remember that, as an employer, you have an obligation to accommodate the religious beliefs of employees and applicants unless to do so would impose an undue hardship on you.

Economic status. Applicants should not be asked about their credit ratings, financial status, bankruptcy proceedings or past garnishment of wages. Is that really what you want to know? For example, instead of asking whether an applicant owns a car, ask: "Do you have a means of getting to work on time each day?"

Union or political affiliation. Don't ask. Screening out job applicants based on their union membership or sympathies is unlawful.

Avoid making promises

Promises made to job applicants may be interpreted by courts as "implied" employment contracts. While interviewing, guard against making promises that won't or can't be kept. Statements to avoid are:
- "You will have a long, rewarding and satisfying career ahead of you."
- "We will pay your moving expenses after one year of service."
- "You will be with us as long as you do your job."
- "You will not be fired without just cause."
- "This is a place where you can stay and grow."
- "In this organization you'll have lots of job security."
- "There are no layoffs within this organization."

Pre-employment testing

Many pre-employment tests are designed to quantitatively measure specific attributes such as an applicant's knowledge, skills, aptitudes or attitudes that are necessary to do a particular job. In theory, with the right test an employer can use a test's scores to *predict* which of the many applicants will perform the best. Tests that fall into this category include:
- tests that measure job knowledge;
- work sample demonstrations conducted under specific guidelines;
- demonstration of physical ability and psychomotor tests;
- intelligence tests; and
- personality tests and interest inventories.

Other tests, such as drug, honesty and genetic testing, are used to eliminate applicants. These tests often function as a part of the employer's security program. These tests include:
- pre-employment physicals and medical information inventories;
- drug testing;
- polygraph or honesty tests; and
- fingerprint processing.

Polygraph tests. Federal law forbids employers from using polygraph tests to screen applicants for employment except in very limited situations. Moreover, the federal polygraph law sets out detailed requirements that must be followed before a test can be given. Many states also have laws forbidding the use of polygraph tests as a condition of employment.

Honesty tests. Pencil and paper honesty tests are generally not prohibited by laws forbidding polygraph testing; however, some states specifically ban the use of written honesty tests as well.

Genetic tests. Some tests are inherently discriminatory while others may be discriminatory because of the manner in which they are administered. The use of genetic tests, for example, poses several legal concerns. While genetic testing may be helpful in identifying applicants who are sensitive to certain chemicals or environmental conditions present in the workplace, the potential for abuse has caused many states to restrict the use of these tests.

In addition, the Equal Employment Opportunity Commission (EEOC) takes the position that employers who discriminate against individuals on the basis of genetic information violate the ADA by regarding those individuals as having impairments that substantially limit a major life activity. Some genetic disorders may also be linked to race or ethnic background. If an employer engages in discrimination based on a genetic trait that is substantially related to a race or ethnic group, the argument can be made that the employer has engaged in unlawful race or ethnicity discrimination. A similar argument can be made for genetic disorders that are linked to sex.

Chapter 2—Choosing your work force

Good intentions or even the absence of discriminatory intent will not redeem testing mechanisms that effectively screen out minority groups and are unrelated to measuring job capability.

Tests that screen out a disproportionately high number of blacks, women or any other group must be validated–that is, proven to be a good predictor of job performance. Moreover, to meet fair employment requirements, each test must be validated for each job. Thus, an industry-wide validation study proving that a test predicts success at welding will not relieve an employer who uses the test from its responsibility to validate the test for its own welding positions.

Best Practices

Pre-employment testing guidelines

Federal equal opportunity guidelines require that employers:
- Measure for adverse impact on protected groups.
- Conduct validation studies where adverse impact has occurred.
- Conform to standards for validation studies.

Pre-employment testing and the ADA

The ADA prohibits an employer from conducting a pre-employment medical examination. A "medical examination" is a procedure or test usually given by a health care professional or in a medical setting that seeks information about an individual's physical or mental impairments or health. Medical examinations include vision tests; blood, urine, and breath analyses; blood pressure screening and cholesterol testing; and diagnostic procedures, such as x-rays, CAT scans, and MRIs.

However, not all procedures and tests are considered medical examinations. Employers are allowed to administer blood and urine tests to determine the current illegal use of drugs, physical agility tests and physical fitness tests.

Employment entrance examination. Once an offer of employment has been made to a job applicant, the employer is permitted to require a medical examination before the applicant begins working. In fact, an employer may condition the employment offer on the results of such examination, provided that:
1. all entering employees must take such an examination regardless of disability;
2. information obtained regarding the medical condition or history of the applicant is collected on separate forms, kept in separate medical files, and is treated as a confidential medical record.

Unlike examinations conducted at any other time, employment entrance examinations need not be job-related or consistent with business necessity. The ADA only guarantees the confidentiality of the information gathered and restricts the use to which an employer may put the information.

Reference and background checks

Reference and background checks can be valuable tools for checking the accuracy of information provided by applicants and for obtaining additional information that was not revealed during the hiring process. Checking past employers, school administrators, and other references does not create a problem under antidiscrimination law unless it is unevenly applied.

If you do not normally check references but decide to do so as to a particular applicant, your decision not to hire that person on the basis of what is learned from the reference check might be seen as discrimination.

Reference and background checks can be an even more valuable tool in preventing negligent hiring claims. An employer's vulnerability to a negligent hiring claim is at its peak at this point. Your organization can be held legally responsible for an employee's wrongdoing on the job if pertinent information that a background check uncovers is ignored or a background check is never even initiated.

Remember Rosa, the applicant who moves around from job to job, never staying in any one position for more than a couple of years? The fact that she has repeated this pattern in three different cities should alert Tim to the possibility that a reference and background check could uncover important information about why Rosa hasn't stayed with the same employer for any length of time. However, if Tim's organization does not normally look into applicants' backgrounds, singling out Rosa for a reference check might be seen as discriminatory.

Worse Case Scenario
Failure to conduct background check

A female graduate student purchased several items of furniture. The furniture was delivered by a van, which prominently displayed the name of the furniture store. The two furniture deliverymen wore shirts with the store name. Shortly after delivering the furniture, one of the deliverymen returned and rang the doorbell. The student, assuming the man was returning on business associated with the furniture, opened the door. The deliveryman entered her home, beat and raped her, and left with her car and valuables.

Ultimately the graduate student received a large jury award because the deliveryman had been previously imprisoned for rape and other violent crimes; however, the furniture store never checked references or conducted a criminal records check. The jury felt the employer had a duty to determine whether or not a potential deliveryman was dangerous to customers.

Solution: If your hires will have contact with customers, especially at their homes or otherwise away from the workplace, be sure you adequately check into their backgrounds.

Privacy concerns. Reference and background checking creates great potential for abuse, however. An applicant's right to privacy must be balanced against an employer's need to know. For this reason, both federal and state law may restrict the collection and/or use of certain types of information. Because of these privacy issues, applicants should be informed that references will be checked and a background investigation will be conducted.

Written authorization should be obtained from an applicant before reference and background checking begins.

Consumer reporting agencies. A credit check is generally appropriate for positions involving access to money or trustworthiness. Federal consumer credit laws restrict the use of consumer reports, however. A permissible purpose is required—and hiring is such a purpose. Applicants must be notified in writing that a report may be required and written authorization from the applicant must be obtained.

Information from the report cannot be used in violation of equal employment opportunity laws. Also, before an adverse action—like a refusal to hire—can be based on a report, the applicant must be furnished with a copy of the report and a summary of consumer rights under the law.

State laws may provide additional restrictions on the use of credit or consumer reports.

Criminal records. Federal and state laws and employee privacy protections are all-important considerations when deciding whether or not to inquire about an applicant's criminal records. Asking about or using *arrest* records as hiring criteria may have an adverse impact on minorities, if they are arrested in percentages higher than their percentage representation in the population as a whole.

Remember, arrest is not conviction. It would be rare for an employer to be able to justify making broad inquiries about arrests.

Chapter 2—Choosing your work force 35

Before asking about criminal records, employers should determine:

- if there is an adverse impact on minority persons;
- if an adverse effect exists, is the absence of a criminal record necessarily related to job performance or warranted by some other business necessity; and
- if a business necessity exists, is there an alternative with a lesser adverse impact?

The EEOC takes the position that an employer must determine whether an applicant actually committed the alleged crime before it can reject an applicant on the basis of an arrest record. This is pretty tough to do. Moreover, employers should refer to state and local laws with respect to whether they can even inquire about an applicant's arrest record.

Using an applicant's *conviction* record is easier to justify. In either case, employment decisions must be based on business necessity.

Consider the nature and gravity of the offense, time elapsed since the occurrence, the nature of the job in question, and any evidence of rehabilitation.

For example, a conviction for marijuana possession 20 years ago with no further criminal history may not be reason to reject an applicant, while a more recent conviction of theft may be.

An applicant's criminal history should be disclosed only to persons with a clearly demonstrable, job-related need to know. All information obtained during the hiring process should be kept confidential and should never be made available to others, even inadvertently.

There are situations when a criminal record check is not only desirable, but also required by law—notably in law enforcement, security, health care and day care work. Many states have laws governing the use of criminal record checks. It is important to know the requirements for the job in question.

State law concerns with criminal record checks. State laws vary greatly on whether or not employers may make criminal record inquires and, if so, how those inquiries may be made. For example:
- Some state laws require employers to conduct criminal record inquiries before employing new employees. These laws most often apply to prison staff, law enforcement, security, public schools, health care workers or day care centers.
- In some states, employers, employment agencies or labor organizations may not inquire on a written application whether a job applicant has ever been arrested or use arrest information or criminal history record information ordered expunged, sealed or impounded as a basis for denying employment or promotion.
- Many states have laws granting employees certain protections regarding criminal record disclosure. While protections vary from state to state, prospective employees generally do not have to disclose any information concerning an arrest, a criminal charge that did not result in a conviction, or any information about convictions that have been pardoned by a governor or in some other manner protected by the courts.
- Where authorized by state law, most states require that applicants be advised that a criminal records check will be done. There may be posting requirements advising prospective applicants that criminal record checks will be conducted. There may also be appeal rights for prospective employees denied employment on the basis of a criminal records check.
- Some states will take legal action against employers who violate the law, including imposing fines for damages and costs.

Medical records. The ADA prohibits an employer from inquiring into an applicant's medical history until after a conditional job offer is made. Because of problems associated with AIDS and genetic testing, many states have laws governing the confidentiality of that information.

ADA and record checks. Because the ADA limits the inquiries an employer can make at the pre-offer stage, employers should make certain public record inquiries only after a conditional offer of employment has been made. For example, the ADA prohibits employers from making inquiries about an applicant's workers' compensation history before an offer of employment is made. After making a conditional job offer, an employer may inquire about a person's workers' compensation history in a medical inquiry or examination that is required of all applicants in the same job category

Military service records. Federal law allows the release of military service records only under very limited circumstances. Available information is generally limited to name, rank, salary, duty assignments and status, and awards.

The job offer

The chief problem at the job offer stage is that, if incorrectly phrased, a job offer may be viewed—first by the applicant and later by a court—as an offer to enter into a binding contract with the applicant. If that's the case, once the applicant accepts the offer, he or she will have good grounds for bringing a lawsuit for breach of contract against your organization if employment is terminated "prematurely."

> In many states, employment is presumed to be at the will of either the employee or the employer, unless they contract with one another to change it. This means that either the employee or the employer can end the relationship at any time for any legal reason—or for no reason at all.

So, unless you intend to enter into a written contract guaranteeing the applicant employment for a set length of time, a job offer should be stated as narrowly and carefully as possible.

> Any statement that alludes to job security can be seen as a promise of job security. Avoid statements like "you will have a long, rewarding career ahead of you" or "you will be with us as long as you do your job."

Under certain circumstances, even quoting an annual salary may imply that the employment is for a year's duration. You may not intend something you say to a candidate to be legally binding, but when a prospective hire relies on your statements, especially by giving up something of value or changing positions, a court may interpret your statements as a binding promise.

✓ Checklist

Avoiding employment contracts

What should you do to avoid inadvertently making employment "contracts?"

☐ **Avoid contractual rights statements.** Avoid all language that would indicate that prospective employees have any contractual rights. A court may view any statement that alludes to job security as a promise. Examine any words or phrases that even remotely imply an offer of employment for a set time period.

☐ **Correct possible misunderstandings.** Review notes of job interview discussions to determine whether any promises were made, implied or otherwise, that need to be corrected in the formal offer letter.

☐ **Disclaim a contract.** Whether written or oral, a job offer should include an explicit statement that "there are no contracts for a particular length or service." Make it clear that either the new hire or the organization may end the relationship at any time and that "just cause is not necessary."

☐ **Do not revoke an offer once made.** A decision to revoke an employment offer may end up being second-guessed by a judge or jury. Either check references and do credit checks *before* making a job offer to a prospective employee, or make the job offer *contingent* upon favorable references and credit.

Immigration recordkeeping requirements

The Immigration Reform and Control Act (IRCA) makes it unlawful for an employer to hire undocumented aliens, or to continue to employ undocumented aliens that were hired after November 6, 1986, which is the date the law became effective.

> An "undocumented alien" is a person who is neither:
> 1. a lawfully admitted permanent resident of the United States, nor
> 2. authorized by law or by the Attorney General to work.

The law also establishes documentation and recordkeeping requirements for all employers, regardless of whether they hire aliens or not. Under the law, employers are required to do two things:

- verify both the identity and the eligibility to work in the United States of all employees hired, and,
- retain an "Employment Eligibility Verification" form (I-9 form) for all employees hired. The form requires employees to attest that they are citizens, lawful permanent residents, or aliens authorized to work. Employers are responsible for ensuring that employees comply with this requirement. Employers must also certify which documents they have examined and have a continuing duty to prepare and maintain the I-9 forms.

Best Practices
Complying with immigration law requirements

- To avoid liability, managers and supervisors must verify and maintain records demonstrating that each employee hired is eligible for employment.
- If a manager requests more or different employment-eligibility documents than are required under the law, or refuses to honor documents offered that reasonably appear to be genuine, he or she will be subject to charges of discrimination.
- In the event that an employee's illegal status becomes known after the initial hiring, it would be unlawful to retain that employee. Knowledge of an individual's lack of authorization for employment includes not only actual knowledge, but also situations where an employer should have known that the individual was not authorized to work.
- An employer who hires employees without documents must fire them if they fail to produce the documents in three days, unless they prove they have ordered them, in which case there is a 21-day extension.
- The law also protects against employment discrimination for legal aliens. Employers with four or more employees may not discriminate on the basis of national origin or citizenship status.
- Seemingly neutral standards that are not supported by business necessity, such as lengthy residence requirements, preferred verification documents, or restrictive language-ability requirements that in fact discriminate may be treated as intentional discrimination, even if the employer didn't intend to discriminate.
- To avoid possible civil rights, age discrimination, and other discrimination suits, avoid having applicants fill out the government's immigration form (Form I-9) during the application process. The I-9 gives the employer access to information, such as age, that should not be used in the

hiring decision. Instead, the employer should wait until the new employee reports for duty at the job site before having him or her complete the Form 1-9.
- ◆ Employers that attempt to avoid immigration law problems by not hiring "foreign-looking" individuals may be violating the nondiscrimination provisions of federal antidiscrimination laws.
- ◆ The law's ban against discrimination because of citizenship status applies to citizens as well as to intending citizens.
- ◆ Citizenship status may be a basis for extending preference to an employee or job applicant over another individual who is an alien. The preference is limited, however, to instances where the two individuals are equally qualified.

Document your decision

While a supervisor or line manager may have authority to hire, it is a good idea for HR to review the hiring decision before an offer of employment is made. A review will help ensure that hiring decisions are based on the ability of a candidate to perform job functions and the process itself is free of bias.

Detailed notes should be kept about why various candidates are rejected or accepted. Notes should be objective, job-related and professional. Copies of written offer letters and documentation of what was said during an oral job offer should always be maintained.

When employment disputes occur, written materials are the most persuasive evidence of what was intended. If a lawsuit later arises, your records will provide an important defense for your hiring choice.

DON'T miss this

HR How-to: EMPLOYMENT LAW

⁇ The Quiz

1. Hiring decisions should not be based on knowledge, skills and abilities that are not listed in the job description. ❏ True ❏ False

2. Federal law expressly prohibits pre-employment inquiries concerning a job applicant's race, religion, sex, national origin, or age. ❏ True ❏ False

3. Once an offer of employment has been made to a job applicant, an employer is permitted to require a medical examination before the applicant starts working. ❏ True ❏ False

4. It is always appropriate to ask job applicants whether they have a high school degree. ❏ True ❏ False

5. Prior to an offer of employment, it is okay to ask disability-related questions as long as they are related to the job. ❏ True ❏ False

Answer key: 1. T; 2. F; 3. T; 4. F; 5. F

Chapter 3

Compensation practices

Overview	44
Equal pay for equal work	45
BEST PRACTICES: Ten steps to a valid merit system	54
Factors other than sex	55
Correcting unequal pay	61
Conduct job analysis	61
Compensating differently based on sex: More than one law applies	63
Other types of prohibited compensation discrimination	65
BEST PRACTICES: Tips for releases to avoid age claims	69
BEST PRACTICES: Compensation	77
Supervisors speak for the company	78
The Quiz	79

Less than five months after Nick was hired as an installment loan lender at one of your organization's branch offices, he was promoted to installment loan officer. At the time of the promotion, Nick received a raise. Although Nick possessed no prior banking or lending experience when he was hired, he did have a four-year college degree. Unfortunately, Nick was terminated several months later.

Patricia, who worked as an installment loan secretary in the same branch as Nick, was promoted to installment loan officer not quite a year after Nick's departure from the bank. Although she had three years of experience in the lending department, Patricia completed only a year and a half of college. She also received a raise at the time of her promotion; however, her new salary was still less than Nick's salary at the time he was first hired. Somehow, Patricia discovered that Nick made more than she does for doing the same job. She is threatening to file a claim with the EEOC, the federal agency charged with enforcing antidiscrimination laws.

HR How-to: EMPLOYMENT LAW

> *Patricia's manager has come to you for advice. He doesn't think Patricia has any reason to complain. After all, she just received a substantial bonus for her work on a recent account. If you combine the bonus with her salary, she will make about the same amount that Nick made when he was promoted to loan officer. Moreover, Nick was terminated months before Patricia was promoted, and right now there aren't even any male loan officers employed in the same branch. But Patricia is still threatening to file a claim if she doesn't get a raise. Should you worry?*

Overview

Employees' wages and hours are regulated under federal law by a number of statutes. The law having the broadest application is the Fair Labor Standards Act (FLSA). Through the FLSA, the federal government sets standards that cover hourly wage rates, overtime pay and equal pay.

Fast FLSA facts

- FLSA covers every employee in the nation (not otherwise exempt) engaged in interstate activities. (It's more likely than not that your workers are covered by the law even if you have a single workplace in only one state.)
- In 2003, the current federal minimum wage rate is $5.15 (but some states may have a higher minimum wage).
- A straight-time workweek of 40 hours is permitted.
- Overtime pay, due when work goes beyond 40 hours in a single workweek, is set at time and one-half of the regular rate.

Many states have enacted their own laws in these areas reaching employees not covered by the federal law, or in some cases, providing more protection than the federal law. Employers obviously need to know the wage-hour laws in states where they do business.

Easier said than done. It has often been said of the FLSA that the law is easy to state, but difficult to apply. So, for instance, it's fairly straightforward to state what the minimum wage is for most workers and that employees must be paid time and one-half their regular rate of pay for all hours worked over 40 in a workweek. That's where the simplicity ends, however.

Chapter 3—Compensation practices

There are many exemptions to these generally stated principles, and as a consequence, there are numerous pitfalls that employers must be aware of to avoid potentially serious financial penalties for failing to compensate their employees properly.

Noncompliance can be very costly. Employers must be aware of the law's requirements to avoid inadvertent violations that could turn into time-consuming investigations and a very large bill for back wages. Additional penalties or damages can be assessed if it can be shown that the employer acted willfully in not complying with the FLSA.

Equal pay for equal work

The Equal Pay Act (EPA), which is part of the FLSA, prohibits sex-based discrimination in compensation practices.

The Equal Pay Act, enacted in 1963, is the oldest of the federal job anti-discrimination laws, yet women workers still earn less pay than their male counterparts.

The Equal Pay Act bars employers from paying male and female employees *in the same establishment* differently for work on jobs that require:
- equal effort;
- equal skill;
- equal responsibility; and
- that are performed under similar working conditions.

Importantly, "working conditions" only have to be similar, while the other factors must be substantially equal.

"Compensation" means any payment made to or on behalf of an employee as remuneration for employment, including:
- salary;
- overtime pay;
- bonuses;
- stock options;
- profit sharing and bonus plans;
- life insurance;
- vacation and holiday pay;
- cleaning or gasoline allowances;
- hotel accommodations;
- reimbursement for travel expenses; and
- benefits.

Example: *An employer provides full temporary disability coverage to its male employees, but it excludes pregnancy and maternity benefits from the coverage it offers to female employees. A female employee alleges that she is being paid an unequal wage because the male employees performing the same job receive full coverage, while she and other female employees do not. The EEOC would find that the employer violated the Equal Pay Act.*

Establishments

Employees who seek equal pay for equal work may compare themselves only with co-workers that are employed within the same "establishment." Usually, each physically separate place of business is a separate establishment. However, it is also possible that two physically separate facilities may be one establishment, or that one facility contains more than one establishment.

If an employer has two or more establishments, nothing prevents it from paying higher rates in one establishment than in another, so long as the establishments are physically separate and operationally distinct.

Job tasks

Conflicts over equal pay frequently involve debate over the significance of differences in job tasks that men and women perform. Generally, jobs are not identical. The sexes may have slightly different assignments, or one sex may have a couple of added duties. Both the nature of the tasks and the amount of time spent on them are important.

In applying the tests of equality to the performance of "jobs," enforcement agents scrutinize the job as a whole and look at the characteristics of the jobs being compared over a full work cycle. This is because the activities and time involved in a job may vary from time to time.

Only substantial equality of job content, not job comparability, is the proper standard for applying the equal pay requirement.

Comparable worker

For there to be an equal pay problem, there must be a comparable worker of the opposite sex to point to. Once that person has been identified, a statistical analysis should be done to determine whether a pay disparity is based on gender.

It is the nature of the job itself that determines substantial equality, not the relative experience of the employee or the quantity or quality of performance. The employee does not have to show that he or she was performing the job as well as someone else as long as there was equal skill, equal effort, and equal responsibility.

Simultaneous employment not required. An equal-pay violation may occur whether or not employees who perform the same work for different pay are employed at the same time. An employer can act unlawfully by paying a replacement employee more money than a member of the opposite sex who has already departed the job.

What's in a title?

The actual day-to-day content of employees' jobs, not their job titles, determines whether the work of male and female employees is substantially equal. Job descriptions are a useful starting point for making this determination.

Job descriptions by themselves are not determinative, however. If the employees perform work that is different than what appears in those descriptions, it is the actual duties that matter.

Job descriptions do not provide an absolute defense against liability for equal pay violations. It is the actual work that counts. However, an employer's conscientious development and review of job descriptions is the best way to avoid potential liability for equal pay violations.

Equal pay considerations provide one reason for employers to take the accuracy of job descriptions seriously. In order to avoid potential equal pay problems, make sure that you identify job tasks in terms of the effort, skills and responsibilities required.

Job descriptions should be compared periodically with employees' actual work. Initial distinctions in job content, however, may become fuzzy over time, as employees work with each other, learn each other's tasks and develop their individual abilities. Equal-pay problems may arise, for example, when a good worker in a low classification is handed increasingly important or complex assignments that may also be performed by higher-paid workers.

Equal skill

Jobs that are not equal in terms of the skills required do not have to be paid at the same rate, even though they may require equal effort, have equal responsibilities and be performed under similar working conditions.

Chapter 3—Compensation practices 49

How do you tell whether jobs are equal as to skills? The relevant criteria for assessing skills are factors like experience, training, education and ability.

There is a difference between skills that are job requirements and the kinds of experience, education, training, ability or productivity that are achieved over and above those requirements and may result in higher pay. For example, a woman and a man may spend a good part of their work time performing the same types of tasks, but they may also perform diversified or additional assignments at other times. Since there is no difference in the skills required for most of their work, it is the relative skill required for the other duties that may be significant.

Greater skills often lead to greater, or at least different, responsibilities. Therefore, the factors of skill and responsibility are necessarily related and often difficult to separate.

Equal effort

Effort must be analyzed in terms of the total requirements of a particular job. It encompasses both physical and mental effort. Physical labor does not automatically lead to a finding that the work of male and female employees is unequal. Rather it is necessary to ask the following questions:

♦ Does the position require exerting equal effort of a different type, such as dexterity or mental effort?
♦ Is the physical effort performed only occasionally, or by only some employees?

The effort of men and women may be substantially equal, even though it is not the same effort. For example, the occasional lifting and carrying required by male porters may be balanced by the kneeling, stooping, reaching or other effort by female maids.

Added physical labor performed by male employees, for example, must be substantial and be performed over a considerable portion of the work cycle, rather than be merely occasional. When some men perform heavier labor, but not others, then a wage differential may be justified only for those who actually exert the extra effort. Paying a higher wage to all men in a "heavy" classification under these circumstances is unlawful.

Equal responsibility

The equal-pay standard applies to jobs that, among other things, require equal responsibility in their performance. "Responsibility" refers to the relative accountability or importance of the obligations, not merely the fact that men and women have different job duties.

✓ Checklist

How to determine equal responsibility

Differences in responsibility often involve one of these job aspects:

- ☐ supervision of other employees;
- ☐ discretion or independent judgment;
- ☐ responsibility for money or other matters of value;
- ☐ consequences of decisions or errors in judgment; and
- ☐ safety or security responsibilities.

Similar working conditions

Work that is substantially equal in skill, effort and responsibility also must be performed under similar working conditions before equal pay is required. The conditions only have to be similar, not substantially equal or identical. The similarity of working conditions relates to "surroundings" or "hazards."

Working conditions do not encompass shift differentials; in other words, the time of day that someone works is not considered a "working condition," all other factors being equal. A shift differential may be a legitimate wage factor other than sex, but the employer must establish that fact. Generally, however, paying a shift differential does not violate the equal pay requirements.

Working in different departments does not necessarily mean that employees are working under different working conditions. However, hazardous conditions may create dissimilar conditions.

Different pay for equal work can be lawful

Different pay for male and female employees who perform equal work is lawful, but only if the difference is based on a:

- seniority system;
- merit system;
- incentive system; or
- factor other than sex.

The seniority, merit and incentive systems must be bona fide systems. They should be adopted without any discriminatory intent and have predetermined criteria for measuring seniority, merit, or productivity. The criteria should be communicated to employees and be consistently and fairly applied to both sexes. And, of course, the system must in fact be the basis for any difference in compensation.

Common "factors other than sex" include job-related education, experience, training, and ability; shift differentials; job classifications systems; and market factors.

Different pay is probably unlawful if the employer is unable to point to a factor other than sex as the reason for it.

A written, communicated plan creates a better environment for consistent application of company policies. Although employers do not have to have formal, written programs to take advantage of these exceptions, failure to communicate a policy to employees may be taken as evidence that none really exists.

Seniority system. No sex discrimination is allowed in differentials paid under a seniority system. A seniority system rewards employees with pay levels that are based, at least in part, on their tenure in their department or with their employer. A seniority system should be distinguished from a practice of paying higher wages to new employees who have greater experience, education or training.

In the absence of a written and communicated policy on seniority, employees may be able to demonstrate that there has been no uniform practice of paying for seniority and, therefore, no real practice at all. A lack of a uniform approach raises suspicions that seniority has been used after-the-fact to justify perpetuation of a gender-based wage differential.

Merit system. Merit systems usually result in some employees in a particular job receiving a higher wage than others in recognition of greater aptitude, interest, diligence, competence and general value to the employer. The Equal Pay Act specifically permits employers to continue to give merit raises without concern that a differential that might result could be found to be unlawful.

When an employer does not have a formal written policy or little evidence of established practice of conducting objective performance reviews, claims of merit-based pay are closely scrutinized.

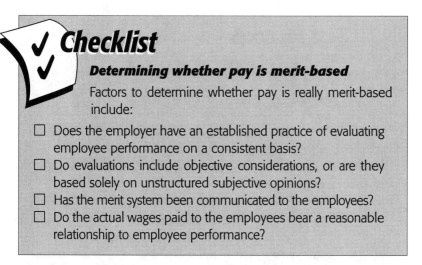

✓ **Checklist**

Determining whether pay is merit-based

Factors to determine whether pay is really merit-based include:

☐ Does the employer have an established practice of evaluating employee performance on a consistent basis?
☐ Do evaluations include objective considerations, or are they based solely on unstructured subjective opinions?
☐ Has the merit system been communicated to the employees?
☐ Do the actual wages paid to the employees bear a reasonable relationship to employee performance?

Evaluation criteria. Objective criteria may include such factors as attendance, error rates, timely completion of assignments and the quantity that is expected for a particular experience level. Other factors, such as quality, initiative, or adding value for customers, necessarily involve some subjectivity. However, identifying specific standards for these factors and noting critical incidents that are related to them create a basis for a more objective analysis in these less tangible areas and are sufficient to establish a merit system for equal pay purposes.

Rating. Employees can be rated at three to five levels of success in satisfying each criterion; for example: (1) exceeds expectations; (2) meets expectations; or (3) does not meet expectations. A point scale, either weighted or unweighted, also may be used to rate overall performance.

> ### 🏅 Best Practices
>
> **Ten steps to a valid merit system**
>
> Structured performance appraisals provide the cornerstone of a merit system that will satisfy equal pay standards. Make sure your merit system follows these steps that will provide essential ingredients for appraisals or evaluations that satisfy equal pay requirements:
>
> - Identify specific job-related criteria on which employees will be judged;
> - Correlate criteria with the overall objectives of the organization;
> - Develop objective standards to the extent possible;
> - Rate employee success in meeting these criteria and previously set goals;
> - Communicate overall merit system and appraisal criteria to employees;
> - Meet with individual employees to discuss results of their evaluations;
> - Negotiate and document individual performance goals for the next review period;
> - Document critical performance incidents during the review period;
> - Offer both praise and constructive criticism when warranted, rather than put it off; and
> - Train supervisors on how to conduct appraisals and how to be objective.

Incentive system. There are many types of systems covered by this exception, including commission sales systems, piece rate systems, and rejection rate systems. To the extent that the compensation received by workers differs because of the commission or piece rate or other such system, the differential may not be unlawful even if it were to result in lower pay for women generally.

Chapter 3—Compensation practices

However, it is important to note that many compensation systems are made up of more than one method of measuring compensation. For instance, direct sales workers are often paid the equivalent of a salary as well as commissions based on quantity of sales. The exception that applies to the commission portion of the sales representative's paycheck would not shield the salary portion from scrutiny under the Equal Pay Act.

Factors other than sex

It is the "any factor other than sex" exception in the Equal Pay Act that generates the greatest dispute. The legislative history of the Equal Pay Act confirms that this exception was included because it would be impossible to list each and every exception.

✓ Checklist

Factors other than sex

Some exceptions intended to be included in the general exception:
- ☐ shift differentials;
- ☐ time of day worked;
- ☐ hours of work;
- ☐ lifting or moving heavy objects;
- ☐ experience;
- ☐ education;
- ☐ training; and
- ☐ ability.

Education, experience and training

Education, experience and training are criteria used to determine whether compared jobs involve equal skill, but they may also be a means to justify a wage differential after equal work has been established. Just because two jobs require equal skill does not mean that an employer cannot recognize an individual's greater education, experience, or training. However, these criteria cannot be used as a pretext for paying one sex a higher wage.

Education, experience or training should be job related, and equal credit must be given to male and female employees for job-related experience, education or training.

Consider Nick and Patricia. Their employer may have a hard time persuading a court that Nick's college degree entitled him to a higher salary as an installment loan officer than Patricia, who had completed one and a half years of college, and also had three years of job-related experience in the lending department. If a degree, for example, is only marginally related to the job, it won't qualify as a factor other than sex and probably cannot support a wage differential.

Additionally, the fact that Nick was terminated before Patricia was promoted and there weren't any other male loan officers working in the same branch at the time Patricia discovered the wage differential won't help their employer if Patricia decides to file a claim. Simultaneous employment isn't required. Remember that equal pay violations can occur whether or not employees who perform the same work for different pay are employed at the same time.

Unrelated job experience. Unrelated job experience may also constitute a factor other than sex for purposes of justifying a wage differential.

> ***Example:*** *Keith, a male shift production supervisor at an automotive engine components plant was paid more than his female counterpart Kira because he had 26 years of experience as a meat market manager in a grocery store, as opposed to Kira's four years of experience running a cleaning service. Neither employee had any prior manufacturing supervisory experience. While managing a meat market and managing a cleaning service might seem equally far afield from overseeing an automobile parts assembly line, because the wage differ-*

ential was based on Keith's extensive supervisory experience, it was based on a factor other than sex and did not offend the Equal Pay Act.

Training programs

Workers employed under training programs are sometimes assigned to various types of work in an establishment. During these assignments, they may be performing the same work as nontrainees of the opposite sex whose wage rate differs. Differentials resulting from training programs do not violate the FLSA equal pay provisions if the same rate is paid to the employees in training status regardless of sex.

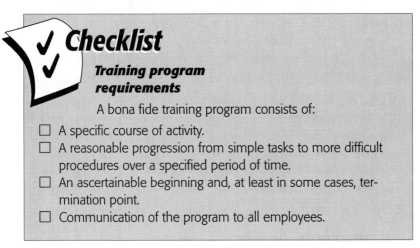

Checklist

Training program requirements

A bona fide training program consists of:
- [ ] A specific course of activity.
- [ ] A reasonable progression from simple tasks to more difficult procedures over a specified period of time.
- [ ] An ascertainable beginning and, at least in some cases, termination point.
- [ ] Communication of the program to all employees.

Shift differentials

Shift differentials do not, as a general rule, violate equal pay requirements. It is even possible for a differential to be paid incidentally only to men and still be lawful. For example, if both men and women work on the same job in an establishment that operates day and night shifts, but only men work on the night shift. In this situation, a night-shift differential *may not* be prohibited.

On the other hand, paying a higher hourly rate to all men on that job for all hours worked—day as well as night hours—because some of the men may occasionally work nights would raise questions as to discrimination based on sex.

Job classification programs

Variations in wage rates as a result of bona fide job classification programs are not unlawful under the equal pay standard if the programs do not discriminate on the basis of sex. However, job classifications or titles standing alone do not justify wage differentials.

Part-time employees

Paying a different wage rate to part-time employees than to full-time employees of the opposite sex does not necessarily violate the federal equal pay provisions, even though both types of employees perform equal work in the same establishment. The differential can be justified on the basis of the difference in working time if the pay practice is applied uniformly to males and females.

This rule applies to employees who only work a few hours a day, or less than 20 hours a week. The wage-rate differential can be based on the difference in the number of hours worked weekly.

Basing a wage differential on the number of hours worked weekly would be suspect if employees of one sex work 30 to 35 hours weekly and employees of the other sex work 40 to 45 hours. Suspicions would arise because different rates for part-time work usually relate to workweeks of 20 hours or less.

Temporary employees

Paying different wage rates to temporary employees, such as those hired during the Christmas season, than to permanent employees performing equal work does not necessarily violate equal pay requirements. No violation results if the following conditions are satisfied:
- ◆ The pay practice is applied uniformly to both men and women.
- ◆ Paying the differential conforms to the nature and duration of the job.
- ◆ Paying the differential conforms to the customary practice in the industry and the establishment.

Chapter 3—Compensation practices

Employment for a period longer than one month will raise questions as to whether the employment is in fact "temporary."

Temporary reassignments—"red circle" rates

For various business reasons, employers sometimes temporarily reassign employees to jobs other than their regular classifications. If the employee's regular job pays a higher rate than the temporary job, payment of the higher rate may be continued during the reassignment without violating the equal pay standard. The rate then becomes a "red circle" rate.

A temporary reassignment also may create the reverse in wage rates—the employee's former rate may be lower than the rate paid to the opposite sex for work involved in the temporary job. Payment of the lower rate may be continued temporarily if the rate is not based on quality or quantity of production. The temporary nature of a reassignment becomes questionable after one month.

If a piece rate is paid to employees of the opposite sex who perform the work to which an employee formerly paid a lower rate is temporarily reassigned, failure to pay the reassigned employee the same piece rate would raise questions of discrimination based on sex.

New hires—entrance rates

Some employers have a range of rates, known as entrance rates, that apply to newly hired employees.

Differentials in entrance rates do not violate the equal pay standard if the factors that determine which rate is to be paid to each new employee are applied equally to males and females.

Paying a newly hired female employee less than the rate paid to a male employee whom she replaces violates the equal pay provisions, even though there are no male employees presently in the establishment who are paid a higher rate for the same work.

Salary retention plans

Some employers permit employees who transfer from one position into another to take their old salary with them, particularly when the transfer results from the elimination of the employee's prior position. Such plans can allow an employer to retain experienced and knowledgeable employees, bolster employee morale and save an employer the cost of training new employees.

> Pay disparities created by an established and uniformly applied salary retention plan are based on a factor other than sex and therefore do not violate the equal pay provisions.

Market rates for employee skills

Market value provides a legitimate basis for a wage differential. However, it is crucial to determine what type of market forces the employer is talking about. Is the employer saying:
- I must beat the salaries being offered by competitors for the same services in order to recruit and retain good employees?
- Or is the employer merely saying something along the lines of: I pay women less because they have less bargaining power, or I must pay male employees more money because they refuse to work for what we pay female employees?

> Paying market rates for new employees presents a question of whether jobs actually are equal in terms of skill or responsibility.

To establish that a pay differential is based on market value, an employer must show that it actually assessed the value of an individual's job-related credentials, and that the differential was based on this assessment rather than on the person's gender. Factors to consider include:
- Did the employer consult with the previous employer about the person's starting and final pay?
- Did the employer determine that the prior salary accurately indicated the person's ability, based on education, experience and other factors?

- Did the employer actually rely on these other factors and the previous pay record?
- If the employer negotiated with a male employee, does it also negotiate with females who are similarly employed?

Correcting unequal pay

What happens if an employer discovers that unequal pay exists in its organization? Compensation discrimination is remedied by raising the pay of the lower-paid employee to equal that of the higher-paid employee.

Unequal pay rates can be equalized only by increases. Reducing rates to accomplish the equalization is against the law.

Similarly, wage differentials cannot be equalized by periodically paying employees of the opposite sex a bonus.

In the situation with Nick and Patricia, the fact that Patricia received a bonus that increased her compensation to approximately the same as Nick's salary did not remedy the equal pay violation. The wage differential can only be remedied by increasing Patricia's salary to equal the salary Nick was making for doing the same work.

Conduct job analysis

Before pegging jobs to a salary range or specific rate of pay, conduct a job analysis. This already may be your standard practice; there are many reasons to do this, and compliance with the equal pay law is just one of them. A job analysis is a systematic process for gathering essential information about a job's duties, qualifications, work conditions and relationship to other work within the organization.

The goals of a job analysis are to develop job descriptions and to document factors that enable management to correlate pay to the relative value of the jobs to the organization.

Pay for particular jobs may be based both on job content and market information about what other employers pay for similar work.

> ✓ **Checklist**
>
> ### Job analysis factors for equal pay
>
> The following examples of data collected in a job analysis clearly pertain to the issue of whether or not jobs are substantially equal.
>
> - ☐ Major job functions, duties and tasks;
> - ☐ skills and competency requirements;
> - ☐ work-related knowledge requirements;
> - ☐ work experience requirements;
> - ☐ education requirements;
> - ☐ training and certification requirements;
> - ☐ mental and physical effort required;
> - ☐ equipment and tools used;
> - ☐ level of supervision over the job;
> - ☐ managerial responsibility;
> - ☐ decision-making authority;
> - ☐ discretion and independent judgment;
> - ☐ budget responsibilities;
> - ☐ performance standards;
> - ☐ descriptions of a typical day;
> - ☐ critical situations faced;
> - ☐ recent changes in the job;
> - ☐ level and type of personal interaction;
> - ☐ confidentiality and security requirements;
> - ☐ environmental and safety factors;
> - ☐ consequences of an error made on the job;
> - ☐ organizational impact of the job;
> - ☐ position in organizational structure; and
> - ☐ career path for job.

Compensating differently based on sex: More than one law applies

When compensation discrimination based on sex is discussed, the Equal Pay Act is not the only federal law involved. Title VII of the Civil Rights Act of 1964 also prohibits employers from paying employees differently based on their sex. Although there is considerable overlap between the two laws, they are not identical. While the Equal Pay Act requires equal pay for equal work, Title VII looks at "similarly situated employees."

WHAT you need to know

> Discrimination in compensation is often subtle and may require close examination. The approach outlined by the EEOC is to identify similarly situated employees and compare their compensation. If there are differences, is there a nondiscriminatory reason for the differences? If the answer is no, then discrimination may be present. Even if there appear to be nondiscriminatory reasons, those reasons should be evaluated to determine whether they actually explain the differences.

Title VII prohibits a broader range of discriminatory practices than does the Equal Pay Act. This means that a violation of Title VII is presumed when there is a violation of the Equal Pay Act, but the reverse is not true. Moreover, in Title VII wage suits involving differing jobs, courts have generally required proof of intentional discrimination. Be aware that employees may have the right to sue under either law.

✓ Checklist

Sex discrimination in compensation: Risk analysis factors

The following series of questions can be used to evaluate the risk of liability associated with wage differentials between employees of opposite sexes. It will guide you through the analysis used by the courts and the EEOC.

Continued on next page

Continued from previous page

Keep in mind that courts evaluate the particular factual context of each case, and the outcome will depend to some extent on what law is applied, including various state laws. Some of the following factors may carry more weight than others. However, all of these areas indicate potential problems that should be considered. Further investigation may be warranted.

- ☐ Do wage differentials exist between the sexes?
- ☐ Is the work equal?
    - ☐ Does the work require equal skill?
    - ☐ Does the work require equal effort?
    - ☐ Does the work require equal responsibility?
- ☐ Is the work performed under similar working conditions?
- ☐ Is the work performed in a single establishment?
- ☐ Is the wage differential based on an exception to the Equal Pay Act?
    - ☐ Is the wage differential based on a seniority system?
    - ☐ Is the wage differential based on a merit system?
    - ☐ Is the wage differential based on an incentive system?
    - ☐ Is the wage differential based on a factor other than sex?
- ☐ Are wage rates applied uniformly within jobs and job classifications?
- ☐ Are any criteria offered to justify wage differentials pretextual?
- ☐ Do facially neutral policies and practices have an adverse impact on one sex?
- ☐ Are employees in differing jobs or job classifications similarly situated?
    - ☐ If so, is there evidence of an intent to discriminate?
    - ☐ Can an intent to discriminate be inferred from the fact of the wage differential itself?
- ☐ Can wage disparities be justified by business reasons?
- ☐ Does state law require pay equity?

Other types of prohibited compensation discrimination

While discrimination in compensation has been most widely challenged on the basis of sex, federal employment laws also prohibit employers from compensating employees differently based on their race, color, religion, national origin, age and disability. The nondiscrimination provisions of the laws also apply to all types of compensation including benefits.

Paid vacations from work, for example, as well as general holidays with pay, cannot lawfully be granted or withheld on the basis of race, color, religion, national origin, or sex. Even when the actual time and money are equal, discrimination can be found in the amount of accommodation to individual preferences.

Older workers

The Age Discrimination in Employment Act (ADEA) bars employers from discriminating on the basis of age in connection with employee compensation.

A wage differential that is based on the assumption that an older worker will be less productive than a younger worker is probably unlawful.

However, the Older Workers Benefit Protection Act, an amendment to the ADEA, allows employers to lawfully provide *different* benefits to older employees in certain circumstances.

"Equal cost" or "equal benefit" required. Although an employer must provide equal benefits to all employees, if the cost of providing a benefit to an older employee is greater than providing the same benefit to a younger worker, the employer can provide smaller benefits to the older worker—as long as the employer spends the same amount for all employees.

WHAT you need to know

Under this "equal cost or equal benefit" rule, employers must either provide equal benefits to both their younger and older employees or they must spend the same amount of money to purchase benefits for both groups of employees, even if the benefits are not equal.

✓ Checklist

Establishing an equal cost defense

The "equal cost" defense does not apply to all benefits, however. According to the EEOC, an employer must show several things in order to raise the equal cost defense:

☐ The benefit is one that becomes more expensive as employees age—for example; life insurance, health insurance, and disability benefits.

☐ The benefit is part of a benefit plan that requires the reduction of benefits as employees age.

☐ The employer spent an equal amount for each of its employees, regardless of age, to purchase the benefit.

☐ The employer reduced benefits for older workers only as much as necessary to equalize the cost of the benefit for each worker.

Special rules apply, however, to certain benefits like health insurance and long-term disability benefits.

Health insurance. Employers are required, under Medicare law, to offer employees who are 65 years and older, and their spouses and dependents, *the same health insurance benefits* as are offered to younger workers and their spouses and dependents.

Early retirement benefits. Early retirement incentive plans may be lawful if they are voluntary and they do not arbitrarily discriminate on the basis of age. An early retirement incentive plan would qualify even if it:

- provides the attainment of a minimum age as a condition for normal or early retirement benefits;
- subsidizes portions of an early retirement benefit; or
- supplements Social Security before the participant reaches the eligibility age to be entitled to benefits.

An employer can lawfully provide cost of living increases only to retirees above a certain age. However, if retirement or health benefits are discriminatorily structured at the time of retirement, the equal benefits or equal cost rule would continue to apply after retirement.

Waivers. Some employers seek protection from potential lawsuits based on age discrimination by requiring employees to sign a waiver form relinquishing their right to sue under the federal law that protects against age discrimination in exchange for enhanced benefits under an exit incentive or early retirement program. The waiver will not be valid, however, unless it is signed voluntarily and with knowledge that certain legal rights are given up.

In cases where an employee might file an age discrimination lawsuit despite having signed one of these waivers, the court will examine the circumstances under which the waiver is signed to determine if the wavier was made "knowingly and voluntarily."

Certain minimum conditions must be met in order for a waiver to be knowing and voluntary.

✓ Checklist

Conditions for proving waiver is knowing and voluntary

An employer must show that these conditions have been met:

- ☐ The waiver is part of an agreement between the employee and employer and written to be understood by the average individual eligible to participate.
- ☐ The agreement makes specific references to rights and claims under the ADEA, which must be specifically referred to by name.
- ☐ The waiver does not waive rights or claims that may arise after the date of the agreement.
- ☐ The waiver is exchanged for valuable consideration in addition to what the employee would already be entitled to receive.
- ☐ The employee is advised in writing to consult with an attorney before signing the agreement.
- ☐ The employee is given at least 21 days within which to consider the agreement; or if a waiver is requested in connection with an exit incentive or other employment termination program offered to a group or class of employees, the individual is given a period of at least 45 days within which to consider the agreement.
- ☐ The employee is given at least seven days following the execution of the agreement to revoke it, and it will not become effective until the revocation period has expired.
- ☐ If a waiver is requested in connection with any exit incentive or other employment termination program offered to a class of employees, the employee must be informed in writing as to any class of individuals covered by the program; any eligibility factors; any time limits for the program; the job titles and ages of all individuals eligible or selected for the program; and the ages of all individuals in the same job classification not selected for the program.

Chapter 3—Compensation practices

In addition, if an EEOC charge or an ADEA lawsuit has been filed, the employee must be given a "reasonable" period of time in which to consider the settlement agreement.

Best Practices

Tips for releases to avoid age claims

One federal court considers the following factors when determining whether a waiver is valid:

- the clarity and specificity of the release language;
- the employee's education and business experience;
- the amount of time the employee had for deliberation about the release before signing it;
- whether the employee knew or should have known his or her rights upon execution of the release;
- whether the employee was encouraged to seek, or in fact received, benefit of legal counsel;
- whether there was an opportunity for negotiation of the terms of the agreement; and
- whether the benefits given in exchange for the wavier and accepted by the employee exceeded the benefits to which the employee was already entitled by contract or law.

Obviously, if an employer is pressuring an employee in any way to sign a waiver and accept exit benefits, as in placing the employee in a "take it or leave it" predicament when offering the benefit package, the waiver will not be upheld.

There are several ways an employer can protect itself against the equal benefit or equal cost rule.

- **Retirement plans.** The Older Worker Protection Act protects subsidized early retirement payments—supplementary payments designed to bridge the gap between early retirement and social security.
- **Severance benefits.** The Act permits an employer to offset severance payments by the value of retiree health benefits and other plan closing "sweeteners" when severance is due to a contingent event unrelated to age—for example, a shutdown or layoff.
- **Long-term disability payments.** Long-term disability packaging (integrating disability benefits and pension benefits) is permitted if the employee elects to receive pension benefits or if the employee is entitled to a pension that will not be reduced because of the employee's age. The value of the pension may be offset after the employee reaches the later of age 62 or normal retirement age. This eliminates the possibility of an employer having to pay both pensions and long-term disability benefits at the same time.

Insurance considerations

There are many types of insurance commonly included in an employment benefit package. As with any type of benefit attached to employment, insurance benefits must be free of discrimination on the basis of race, color, religion, sex, or national origin and may not discriminate against employees 40 years of age or older.

In setting the amount of contribution required of employees, risk should be calculated on an individual basis. Calculating risk on the basis of an actuarial distinction based entirely on sex can be discriminatory. Even though it may be true that women as a group live longer than men and that, as a result, benefits are likely to cost more for women than for men, it is not lawful to attribute this group characteristic to each individual woman.

The principle that risk should be calculated on an individual basis applies to employers' group medical and other insurance as well as to life insurance.

Head-of-household rule. An employer is not required to provide insurance coverage for dependents of employees, but if such benefits are provided they must be equally available to male and female employees. In many cases, a practice of offering family insurance benefits to employees only if they earn more than half of the family's combined income amounts to unlawful sex discrimination. Where an employer conditions benefits available to employees on whether the employee is the head of household or the principal wage earner in the family unit, the overall implementation of the plan will be closely scrutinized.

Head-of-household insurance practices can be lawful if they are shown to be justified by overriding business considerations.

Pregnancy

Employers are required by the Pregnancy Discrimination Act of 1978 to treat pregnancy, childbirth, and related medical conditions the same as other medical conditions for purposes of employment benefits

The EEOC takes the position that maternity, pregnancy, and abortion-related benefits are "wages" under the Equal Pay Act.

Thus, an employer may not legally provide full temporary disability coverage to male workers but deny pregnancy and maternity benefits to female workers who do the same work.

In addition, it is unlawful for an employer to provide full temporary disability coverage to all of its workers and their spouses but exclude pregnancy and maternity benefits from the coverage of spouses of male workers.

Any attempt to charge higher premiums to female employees for medical insurance on the basis of the higher potential for claims because of pregnancy-related medical costs would be sex discrimination.

Health plans that don't cover the cost of prescription contraceptive drugs for women while covering a number of other preventive drugs, devices, and services may be unlawful discrimination on the basis of sex and pregnancy. A number of state laws now require private insurance coverage of contraceptives, and a few courts have found the failure to cover women's prescription contraceptives to be discriminatory, but the issue is still unsettled.

Employees with disabilities

Employers can provide insurance plans that comply with existing federal and state insurance requirements, even if the terms of those plans have an adverse affect on people with disabilities. However, the provisions can't be used as a subterfuge to evade the purposes of the Americans with Disabilities Act (ADA).

Here are the rules on employer-provided health insurance and disability-related coverage:

- Where an employer provides health insurance through an insurance carrier that is regulated by state law, it may provide coverage in accordance with accepted principles of risk assessment and/or risk classification, as required or permitted by such law, even if this causes limitations in coverage for individuals with disabilities.
- Self-insured plans that are not subject to state law may provide coverage in a manner that is consistent with basic accepted principles of insurance risk classification, even if this results in limitations in coverage to individuals with disabilities.

Limits on procedures and treatments. Employers can offer insurance policies limiting coverage for certain procedures, drugs or treatments, as long as an employee with such a condition is not denied coverage for other conditions because of the existence of the excluded or capped condition.

Suppose an employer's insurance policy limits the number of blood transfusions per year. If a hemophiliac exceeds this treatment limit, the employee may not be denied coverage for other conditions because of the existence of the hemophilia.

Limitations on the number of x-rays or noncoverage of experimental drugs and procedures or elective surgery is common. However, these types of limitations must apply to people with or without disabilities. Universal limits or exclusions from coverage are acceptable as long as the medical procedures that are limited are not exclusively, or nearly exclusively, utilized for the treatment of a particular disability. This is true even though the exclusion may have an adverse effect on individuals with certain disabilities.

__Example:__ The XYZ Company health insurance plan limits the benefits provided for the treatment of any physical condition to a maximum of $25,000 per year. One of XYZ's employees files a discrimination charge alleging that the $25,000 cap violates the ADA because it is insufficient to cover the cost of treatment of her cancer. However, the $25,000 cap does not single out a specific disability, discrete group of disabilities, or disability in general. It is, therefore, not a disability-based distinction. If it is applied equally to all insured employees, it does not violate the ADA.

Limits related to conditions. Health plans may provide differing levels of coverage for different conditions so long as such plans apply equally to disabled and nondisabled employees and the distinctions are not disability-based.

> **Example:** *XYZ Company would be violating the ADA if it applies a "neutral" health insurance plan limitation on "eye care" only to an employee seeking treatment for a vision disability, but not to other employees who do not have vision disabilities.*

Monetary caps that are different for some conditions than others are prime examples of permissible distinctions. However, employers invite controversy when they adopt health-related insurance distinctions that are based on disability.

This does not mean that employers can never include terms or provisions based on disability. Disability-based insurance plan distinctions are permitted, but only if they are:

- bona fide;
- based on underwriting risks, classifying risks, or administering such risks that are based on or not inconsistent with state law; and
- not being used as a subterfuge or excuse to evade the purposes of the ADA.

Analysis of policy coverage. When considering a policy limitation or exclusion, employers should go through the following analysis:

Is the distinction disability-based? If the distinction in coverage is not disability-based, there is no violation of the ADA—provided that the distinction applies to individuals with or without disabilities. A term or provision is "disability-based" if it singles out:

- a **particular disability** such as deafness, AIDS, or schizophrenia;
- a **discrete group of disabilities**, such as cancers, muscular dystrophies, or kidney diseases; or
- **disability in general**, such as noncoverage of all conditions that substantially limit a major life activity.

Is the distinction bona fide based on underwriting risks? If the distinction is disability-based, it may be justified through accepted principles of risk assessment and/or risk classification, as required or permitted by state law or in a manner that is consistent with basic accepted principles of insurance risk classification.

Is the distinction a subterfuge to evade the purposes of the ADA? Employers are free to establish and observe the terms of a bona fide benefit plan, including disability-based terms, that are not a "subterfuge to evade the purposes" of the ADA.

Disability-based insurance distinctions that are a "subterfuge" are ones that intentionally discriminate on the basis of disability—disability-based disparate treatment that is not justified by the risks or costs associated with the disability.

Proving a policy doesn't violate the ADA

Should an EEOC investigator decide that a challenged health insurance term or provision is a disability-based distinction, employers can take the following actions:

- Collect evidence that the health insurance plan is a bona fide plan.
- If the health insurance plan is an insured plan (as opposed to a self-insured plan), find evidence that the plan is not inconsistent with any applicable state law(s).
- Accumulate evidence relevant to any business or insurance justification that is offered to justify the disability-based insurance distinction. This evidence needs to be specific and detailed.

These are the types of evidence needed to prove that the health insurance plan is either a bona fide insured plan that is not inconsistent with state law, or a bona fide self-insured plan. This evidence also helps establish that the challenged disability-based distinction is not being used as a subterfuge.

Retirement and pension plans

An employer must provide like retirement and pension benefits to similarly situated employees without regard to race, color, religion, age, sex or national origin. For example, if an employer provides benefits to male employees, it must provide the same benefits to similarly situated female employees.

Like insurance contributions, a retirement plan or pension plan that requires higher contributions by female employees than by male employees is probably going to be unlawful sex discrimination, even though the difference is based on actuarial tables.

Service v. disability retirement. The EEOC takes the position that it is permissible under the ADA for employers to provide a disability retirement plan with lower levels of benefits than the same employer's service retirement plan.

The distinction is that the two plans constitute two separate benefits that serve different purposes: A disability retirement plan provides a lifetime income for an employee who becomes unable to work because of illness or injury without regard to age, while a service retirement provides a lifetime income for employees who have reached a certain age and who have completed a specified number of years of service with the employer.

Neither of these plans make distinctions based on whether or not an individual is covered under the ADA.

Be aware that violations will occur under either type of plan when an employer treats a qualified individual with a disability less favorably because of that individual's disability, or when an employer denies persons covered by the ADA access to a plan that would be available to persons not covered by the ADA. In such a case, the EEOC will seek relief for the aggrieved persons unless the employer shows that it did not act on the basis of the disability or proves that the plan is sheltered by the ADA's defense for certain bona fide employee benefit plans.

Best Practices

Compensation

The Office of Federal Contract Compliance Programs has identified Best Practices from Award Winning Affirmative Action Programs that describe practices promoting equal employment opportunity and affirmative action. The following steps are ones that employers have used that promote best practices in compensation.

- **Step one:** Conduct a self-audit.
- **Step two:** Correct any of the problem areas identified by the self-audit.
- **Step three:** Create a set of procedures and practices for ensuring that all decisions on compensation in the future are based on job-related criteria that are consistent with business necessity and are applied uniformly and consistently to each and every pay decision.

Some best practices to ensure fairness in compensation programs that have been used by employers are:

- Conducting a job evaluation survey for each job in the facility to establish what the labor market in your area is paying for these occupations. Employers may choose to use "benchmark" positions for the sake of efficiency and economy.
- Training each individual who makes starting salary decisions in how to apply the company policy on starting salaries.

Where pay is tied to performance ratings:

- Developing a performance rating system, with measurable criteria, that clearly differentiates between levels of performance.
- Ensuring that any subjective elements, such as "initiative," are operationally defined by providing concrete examples of what the element means.
- Ensuring that all rating managers are trained in the consistent and uniform application of the elements in the assessment of an individual worker's performance.
- Examining the impact of compensation decisions on minorities and women to assure that they do not have disparate impact on either of these groups.

Supervisors speak for the company

Supervisors' promises to employees may be interpreted by courts as enforceable employment contracts.

Statements made by supervisors can be directly attributed to their organization. Supervisors are considered to be agents of the organization. This means that any statements made by a supervisor can be attributed to the employer and used as evidence to show that a company acted improperly. Thus, HR must make certain that supervisors know to be careful that their statements relate only to their job of managing people to meet company goals.

While it is the responsibility of a supervisor to know what the benefits policy of the employer is, it is not the supervisor's job to handle inquiries regarding that policy.

Train supervisors to direct questions about benefits first to the employee benefit handbook and then to the benefits administrator.

The supervisor should make sure that each employees has a copy of the benefits plan and keep employees informed about any changes in the plan. However, the supervisor should in no way attempt to interpret the plan's provisions for employees. Any such interpretation could become an enforceable oral modification to that plan, resulting in real problems for the employer.

The Quiz

1. Which one of the following statements is not true?
   a. Different pay for male and female employees who perform equal work is lawful, but only if the difference is based on a seniority, merit or incentive system, or some factor other than sex.
   b. Employers can resolve problems of unlawful pay differentials by lowering the wages of the higher-paid workers, or discrepancies can be fixed by paying the lower-paid workers a bonus.
   c. The actual day-to-day content of employees' jobs, not their job titles, determines whether the work of men and women is substantially equal.

2. Jobs that are not equal in terms of the skills required do not have to be paid at the same rate, even though they may require equal effort, have equal responsibilities and are performed under similar working conditions. ❏ True ❏ False

3. The fact that a male employee's additional duties involve safety or security responsibilities is not sufficient to justify a wage differential. ❏ True ❏ False

4. Employers can never provide different benefits to older employees. ❏ True ❏ False

5. Health plans may provide differing levels of coverage for different conditions so long as the plans apply equally to disabled and nondisabled employees and the distinction are not disability based. ❏ True ❏ False

Answer key: 1. b; 2. T; 3. F; 4. F; 5. T

Chapter 4

Performance appraisals

Create a record 82
Keep it objective 85
Keep it honest 89
    BEST PRACTICES: Accurate appraisals
    are best defense against lawsuits 90
Use performance appraisals for selection 91
Reasons why appraisals are not effective 92
    BEST PRACTICES: Tips for avoiding litigation 97
Tie performance appraisal to other policies 97
Maintain "need-to-know" basis for access 100
    BEST PRACTICES: Tips for making negative
    appraisals positive 100
The Quiz 101

> Marty, a valued manager in your organization, wants to terminate Sandy, a 55-year-old project manager. For the last year, Marty has been coaching Sandy in order to improve her performance. Sandy has always had a problem meeting project deadlines, even though they have been quite reasonable. Sandy does not appear to have the organizational skills required for the job. Otherwise, she has followed procedures and never engaged in misconduct of any kind. Sandy's lack of performance improvement is the only reason she should be terminated.
>
> Six months ago, however, Sandy filed a "whistleblower" complaint with the EPA against your organization. No fines were assessed but negative publicity resulted. You just looked in Sandy's personnel file for documentation that might support Marty's decision. Except for Sandy's most recent evaluation where Marty wrote "getting too old to do the job," past performance evaluations show good, average performance and pay raises.
>
> Marty is in a big hurry to get a new employee in to get the projects back on track. But you're worried that terminating Sandy will expose the organization to more bad publicity, not to mention a possible lawsuit for retaliatory discharge or age discrimination. Is there anything you can do?

Create a record

Good performance appraisal involves setting goals for employees to meet and then providing regular feedback on how employees are doing in meeting those goals. Performance appraisals serve to document an employee's awareness of performance standards and that the employee was given an opportunity to improve performance problems. They also identify good performers and bad performers. Ultimately, performance appraisals provide the written record to support a decision to fire someone who has not responded to attempts to improve performance.

Performance appraisals are a tool that supervisors can use to manage effectively. They are not paperwork for the HR department. When done correctly, performance appraisals achieve two important management functions:

1. *Improve employee performance.*
2. *Create a record of performance.*

Are there legal requirements for performance appraisals?

No legal requirement to conduct performance appraisals. There is no law that requires an employer to provide performance appraisals. If an employer does not commit to providing appraisals, there is no obligation to do so. Many courts have made clear that an employee does not have a right to a performance appraisal.

However, if an employer commits to provide performance appraisals, it may establish a contractual obligation to do so.

Performance appraisal systems are often described in employee handbooks. If the language used to describe a performance appraisal system is specific enough, it might be viewed as a promise to conduct job reviews on a regular basis. In some states, such language could create a binding contract. Some experts recommend that any discussion of performance appraisals include a discussion of your organization's employment-at-will policy.

If you do performance appraisals, you may not discriminate.
Further, if an employer provides appraisals, the employer must comply with applicable laws and regulations.

Federal and state laws prohibiting employment discrimination are the main sources of legal concern for performance appraisal. Employees may allege that a promotion denial, layoff, discharge or compensation action was illegally influenced by factors such as the employee's race, disability, sex or age.

Employers typically will turn to past performance appraisals to justify the action. If performance appraisals are not well documented or are inconsistently applied, the employer's defense is weakened or destroyed.

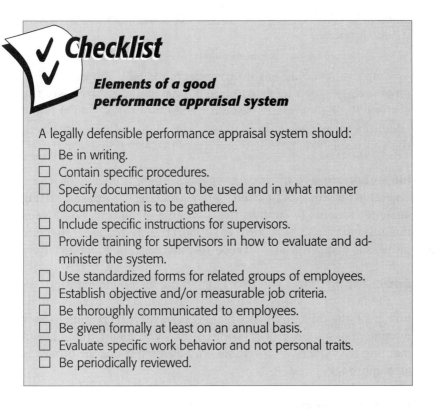

✓ Checklist
Elements of a good performance appraisal system

A legally defensible performance appraisal system should:
- ☐ Be in writing.
- ☐ Contain specific procedures.
- ☐ Specify documentation to be used and in what manner documentation is to be gathered.
- ☐ Include specific instructions for supervisors.
- ☐ Provide training for supervisors in how to evaluate and administer the system.
- ☐ Use standardized forms for related groups of employees.
- ☐ Establish objective and/or measurable job criteria.
- ☐ Be thoroughly communicated to employees.
- ☐ Be given formally at least on an annual basis.
- ☐ Evaluate specific work behavior and not personal traits.
- ☐ Be periodically reviewed.

There are several major constraints the law places on performance appraisal systems, including:

Use of subjective criteria. A rating system that is subjective is not necessarily a problem. For example, ratings on traits such as leadership are subjective. Further, rating characterizations such as above average are also subjective. These factors are not in and of themselves unfair.

What is prohibited is when a standard or a measure of a standard is unfairly applied, or there is no standard. Standards, or lack of standards, that produce disparate treatment in employment decisions such as promotions, compensation or discipline, are also prohibited.

Employers should ensure that raters (usually, the employees' direct mangers or supervisors) do not have total control over the system. Rating standards should be set by others, and training should be provided on how to rate and apply ratings. Moreover, the appraisal system itself should be periodically reviewed.

Inappropriate use of documentation. There are ways in which objective records can be used inappropriately. For example, using absentee records to support the discharge of minority employees but not using the same records to support the discharge of other employees is inappropriate. All records must be applied uniformly.

Documenting "after the fact". Searching for documentation "after the fact" or to support an adverse decision is generally unfair but, given the difficulty many managers have with creating proper documentation, more of a problem than you might think. Documenting trivial actions for some employees but not for others is also improper.

Infliction of emotional distress. The use of a bona fide performance appraisal system to criticize employees' behavior generally will not support a claim that a negative appraisal caused emotional distress. If the criticism is extreme or outrageous, intentionally reckless, intended to hurt or cause emotional distress, and a reasonable person would feel severe discomfort from the criticism, then it is not acceptable.

> Teach managers and supervisors that effective performance appraisal is a tool, not a weapon.

In general, any personnel action such as discipline or discharge may be defended from challenge if it is done for a legitimate business justification. Poor performance is one such business justification.

In any lawsuit that challenges an adverse personnel action, the first piece of evidence that an employee's attorney will ask for is the employee's past performance appraisals. If the case goes to trial, those appraisals will be enlarged and put on display for a jury to scrutinize. They will also take them back into the jury room to be reviewed in detail. It is, therefore, essential that performance appraisal be done fairly and consistently.

Keep it objective

Relevance and objectivity. There are two basic rules for effective performance appraisals:

- ◆ Descriptions of performance must be based on factors that are relevant to performance of the job.
- ◆ Performance must be described in objective terms and be measured in terms of behavior or actions on the job that can be observed by the supervisor. Subjective, vague or overly broad descriptions such as "poor attitude" or "no initiative" should have no place in a performance appraisal. Often these are conclusions on the part of the supervisor and not actual descriptions of performance.

Performance should be measured in terms of behavior or action that can be objectively seen.

Performance appraisal systems fail when they are based on subjective opinions about how a person is performing.

A manager should not base a performance appraisal on a person's attitude or what the manager thinks is going on inside the person's head.

This does not mean that an employee cannot be disciplined for a "bad attitude," or rewarded for a "good attitude." What this means is that behavioral examples of what constitutes a good or bad attitude should be spelled out.

> **Example:** *Providing good customer service is a common goal upon which employees are evaluated. But it is not enough to state that an employee's goal is good customer service. Effective performance evaluation requires that objective, observable behavior be spelled out with examples of what constitutes good customer service. Thus, good customer service might require that each customer be greeted within 10 seconds and thanked after every purchase. These are actions that can be observed and documented.*

Worst case scenario
Evaluation based on subjective performance criteria

An African American employee alleged that his discharge was racially motivated. The employer countered that performance evaluations established that the employee was unfit for the position. The court ruled that the employer's subjective performance criteria did not establish that the employee was incapable of doing his job.

Negative evaluations of the employee were couched in such terms as "lacks a sense of priorities" and "lacks initiative." Noting that subjective evaluations are more susceptible of abuse and likely to mask pretext, the court found the company could not initially establish that the employee was unqualified for the job by using such performance evaluations.

Solution: Performance appraisals should describe performance in objective terms and must be based on factors that are relevant to the performance of the job. Moreover, a performance appraisal should contain supporting examples of the employee's deficiencies or conduct.

Here are some examples of how ineffective vague conclusions can be turned into more objective specific descriptions of on-the-job activity.

Subjective	Objective
Lacks customer orientation.	Does not greet customers quickly.
Chronically absent.	Absent six workdays in last month.
Does not care about quality.	Has error rate of 10%.
Lacks interest in work.	Does not complete assignments.

Remember Marty, the valued manager who repeatedly gave Sandy good, average performance appraisals? There are two potential legal problems with recommending Sandy's termination.

First, the fact that Sandy reported what she thought was an environmental violation could raise the issue of a possible retaliatory termination. Even if all the documentation Marty created supported his decision to terminate Sandy, she is a whistleblower who may be entitled to protection from retaliation. The fact that Sandy filed a complaint did not influence Marty, but the retaliation issue could come up. How could you, as an employer, prove it did not influence Marty?

Secondly, of course, the documentation does not support the decision to terminate Sandy. Although Sandy consistently failed to meet her deadlines, Marty never mentioned this deficiency in his evaluations of Sandy. Not only are the past appraisals inadequate to support Marty's decision, they might suggest that there was another reason for Sandy's termination.

Marty's note on Sandy's most recent performance appraisal stating that she was "getting too old to do the job," could land Marty's employer in court, defending an age discrimination lawsuit.

Appraisals that are not consistent with the employer's stated reason for taking an adverse employment action can be enough to get a case before a jury.

Although poor performance is a legitimate business reason for terminating an employee, Marty based his appraisal of Sandy on his subjective opinion about why Sandy was failing to meet her deadlines. As a result, terminating Sandy at this point could be costly.

Ensuring effective performance appraisals. There are several ways for an employer to try to ensure that performance appraisals are objective, including:

- Instituting an automatic review of performance appraisals by the next highest level of management with sign-off.
- Requiring random audits of appraisals for EEO compliance by the equal employment opportunity staff to ensure that performance reviews do not impact adversely on one group of protected employees.
- Providing appeal procedures when an employee disagrees with the appraisal.
- Providing an area on the appraisal for an employee to indicate disagreement. HR staff should read and sign-off on every appraisal before filing. If the employee has raised issues, HR can then follow-up.

Keep it honest

Nobody wants to be the bearer of bad news. A common problem with performance appraisals is that the supervisor sugarcoats a negative performance appraisal. It's HR's responsibility to teach supervisors that softening a negative performance appraisal can result in the point not getting across to the employee that he or she is doing a poor job.

An employee who is unaware that a performance problem exists cannot take steps toward improvement.

Most of all, performance appraisals must be an accurate reflection of what an employee did on the job. Appraisals that do not accurately show a record of poor performance can be used against the organization. Employees' lawyers and government agencies will quickly point to an appraisal that doesn't mention performance problems to refute a supervisor's contention that someone was disciplined or fired for poor performance.

Accurate appraisals allow an organization to counteract allegations that someone was unlawfully disciplined because of his or her age, race, sex or other protected trait.

Performance appraisals need to set forth more than conclusory statements as to deficiencies or conduct. The appraisal should include supporting examples for any deficiency, along with suggested action for improvement of performance. In that way, the manager is forced to evaluate more objectively the employee's total performance without the tendency to overrate.

Best Practices

Accurate appraisals are best defense against lawsuits

The following examples show how accurate performance appraisals can help companies defend against lawsuits alleging that a termination was unlawful:

- A 60-year-old employee is laid off. He files a lawsuit claiming that he was chosen for termination because of his age. The employer uses past performance ratings to show that the employee was one of the three lowest performers chosen for layoff. The court agrees that the performance ratings stating that the employee needed to improve his work provided a legitimate business reason for the discharge.

- A 53-year-old manufacturing manager filed a lawsuit alleging he was fired because of his age. The manager argued that his plant's production performance was excellent in the past and any recent decline in production was due to general economic conditions. The employer was able to show, however, that the decision to fire was based on the manager's inability to get along with people. Evaluation records showed that the manager had been repeatedly counseled and warned about his inability to communicate and get along with superiors and subordinates. The court found that those appraisals showed that the manager was not performing up to his employer's expectations.

- A black sales representative claimed he was fired due to his race. The company successfully defended the suit by showing that the employee did not respond to a performance improvement program. The program pointed out specific deficiencies in performance and set out specific goals for improvement. The goals included objective descriptions of improved selling techniques, the elimination of customer complaints, better organization and planning, and utilization of more sophisticated sales techniques.

Use performance appraisals for selection

Performance appraisals can be viewed as a "test" and/or a selection device. If disproportionately higher numbers of minorities or females are excluded from promotions or given lower pay increases, or if higher numbers are laid off, the employer will still need to show that the performance appraisal is a valid measure of a person's performance.

As a general rule, the criteria used to evaluate employees must be job related.

Document all performance problems regularly on appropriate appraisal or progressive discipline forms. Provide the employee with a copy immediately.

> A precise format for conducting an evaluation leads to more thorough, accurate recording of information. Informality, on the other hand, may lead to claims of discrimination.

✓ Checklist

Objective and subjective performance criteria

In performance appraisals, the following criteria have been found to be reasonably objective:

- ☐ Ability to plan, develop, initiate, and carry through a project with general guidance
- ☐ Education
- ☐ Experience
- ☐ Supervisory experience
- ☐ Personality

Criteria that have been found to be too vague and subjective include:

- ☐ Adaptability
- ☐ Bearing
- ☐ Demeanor
- ☐ Manner
- ☐ Social behavior

DON'T miss this

Promptly evaluate nonproductive employees. When managers tolerate an employee with a performance problem for months and then suddenly give the employee a negative evaluation and ultimately fire him or her, the employee may claim that the action was arbitrary or discriminatory and may be able to show that no opportunity for improvement was given.

If immediate supervisors are to recommend employees for promotion, the supervisor should be given instructions, in writing, as to what qualities are sought for the new position.

✓ Checklist

Lawful bases for denying promotion

The following bases for denying advancement to candidates for promotion have been considered lawful:

☐ Lack of requisite skills.
☐ Failure to pass a valid written test that reasonably gauges ability to perform work in question.
☐ Ineligibility to participate in a preparatory training program.
☐ Refusal to accept required schedule changes.
☐ Poor disciplinary record.
☐ Poor attendance record.
☐ Unwillingness to take on extra assignments.
☐ Unsatisfactory prior work record.

Reasons why appraisals are not effective

Objective standards for measuring performance are the cornerstone of an effective performance appraisal system. But once valid standards are set, an ineffective performance appraisal many times can be traced to the person who is conducting the appraisal—usually the immediate supervisor or manager.

Chapter 4—Performance appraisals

> Supervisors who are rating all their employees satisfactory are not making the tough performance distinctions required for an effective performance evaluation system. Supervisory training can be the key to effective performance appraisal.

Here are some of the reasons why supervisors do not conduct effective performance appraisals and what can be done about them.

Training. When a supervisor performs poorly in conducting performance appraisals, it may not result from lack of effort or interest. HR needs to take a good look at whether the supervisor's poor performance is caused by improper or inadequate training that leaves the supervisor unable to perform the job.

> If your supervisors are doing a poor job of performance appraisal, look first at the support and training they have received. Remember training is the solution to a performance problem if the employee lacks the basic skills or knowledge to do a job.

Guilt. Many supervisors feel uncomfortable exercising managerial power over others when it can have adverse consequences in terms of pay or job security. Or they feel guilty about criticizing performance and hurting a subordinate's feelings. Supervisors must work through these emotions. Hurt feelings are an unavoidable side effect of criticism, but it is often the first step to changing employee behavior and moving down the path to where criticism will not have to be heard again.

Lack of accountability. Supervisors often conduct ineffective performance appraisals because they are not rated on their ability to give feedback. Conducting effective performance appraisal should be written into a supervisor's job description. Make it clear that part of the supervisor's job duties and responsibilities is to set goals for employees and counsel them on performance relative to those goals. Base accountability on the supervisor's exercise of skill in coaching activities designed to develop people and improve their performance.

Ineffective application of standards. Overrating can also be a problem; sort of like grade inflation. This occurs, for example, when poor employees are rated as marginally competent, marginal employees are rated as satisfactory, satisfactory employees as above standard, and good employees are rated excellent.

If an employee is discharged for poor performance but has constantly been overrated as an average performer, past performance appraisals can be used against the organization.

The employee can reasonably argue that for years his performance has been rated satisfactory, and suddenly he is being terminated. Obviously, it can't be because of his performance because his evaluations have been satisfactory. Therefore, the employee assumes the termination was for some illegal reason.

Teach supervisory personnel to include in performance appraisals supporting examples for any significant comments, especially for any deficiency, along with suggested action for improvement of performance.

The halo effect. The "halo effect" is the tendency to generalize from a single characteristic or from the supervisor's general impression of the person being rated. Being aware of a tendency to generalize will help some supervisors keep the halo effect to a minimum. Some supervisors may also tend to rate a workforce generally high or low because of self-serving reasons, such as blaming problems on the caliber of the workforce or demonstrating how effective the supervisor is.

If all rating in a work unit or department is generally uniform, ask the next level of management to compare the ratings with objective data concerning the productivity, error rates and production of the department.

Clustering around the center. Here the rater tends to avoid both ends of the scale and rates subordinates around the middle mark. If there is scarcely any difference between the best and worst performers, the point of the evaluation is to a considerable extent lost. Sometimes this type of error is the result of supervisors' ignorance about their subordinates' performance, but it can also be caused by the way an organization itself deals with the ratings.

Leniency or strictness. Some supervisors give constantly high scores and some give constantly low scores. This may be the result of varying standards and interpretations. HR needs to reach agreement in advance with management about standards and expectations, which may help to overcome this problem.

Over-concentration on recent error or success. There is a tendency to rate people on the most easily remembered behavior, often the most recent, which may not be characteristic of the entire appraisal cycle.

Teach supervisors instead to use a critical incident method, which documents critical incidents as they happen, to help overcome this problem.

Difference in raters. If there are several different appraisers within an organization, make allowance for different standards of judgment that appear over time. It is, of course, better to reduce the differences, but be realistic; HR may simply need to compensate for the differences.

Lack of information. Inaccurate appraisals may result from the appraiser having insufficient information about job performance or the job itself. Coach supervisors to base appraisals as much as possible upon a representative sampling of performances. Judgments based on hearsay, random behavior, or no information at all usually are invalid.

Reluctance to judge. Like most people, it is common for supervisors to feel some reluctance when asked to record unfavorable observations about others, particularly when faced with having to explain the unfavorable rating to the employee. Sometimes this reluctance is the result of inexperience; sometimes it arises from the natural wish to be liked by one's subordinates.

Training supervisors in ways of handling unfavorable appraisals often helps overcome the anxiety surrounding conducting a negative appraisal. HR will lessen the problem by coaching supervisors on ways to ensure the appraisal is based on job performance or on objective goals.

Favoritism. Supervisors are human and make subjective decisions. It is difficult to continue to exercise power for the company but not to use that power for personal use. Whether it is favoring subordinates that appeal to the supervisor, punishing subordinates that the supervisor does not like or both, supervisors are put in positions that are personally difficult and create risk for the company.

The culture, climate, ethics and values of the company and the performance system itself all can act to ensure that supervisors conform to the company's needs and objectives, even when different from their own.

At the same time, failing to provide an objective support system and to audit behaviors may result in costly errors. In some situations, favoritism gives way to bias and prejudice. Companies must be careful that supervisors do not take actions based on bias and prejudice. Typically, companies that have managers who discriminate will be liable for that discrimination.

Best Practices

Tips for avoiding litigation

To avoid litigation and to evaluate professionally, avoid the following:

- Don't evaluate without an objective standard for comparison.
- Don't let a person's length of service affect the evaluation.
- Don't let personal feelings influence or bias the evaluation.
- Don't evaluate employees whose work is not known to you.
- Don't rate with any emotion.
- Don't rush the evaluation process.
- Don't rate most factors or most people the same.

Tie performance appraisal to other policies

While many policies affecting the employment relationship can be implemented without making changes in other policies, employee evaluation is, for the most part, pointless unless it is closely tied to several other policies.

Job analysis. Planning an evaluation or performance appraisal system may mean, for example, backing up several steps and taking a hard look at your organization's jobs.

> **Example:** *Is a customer service representative expected to spot and correct spelling errors in a customer's account, or simply to input accurately new material from the customer? Is courtesy an element of the representative's job? How much time should be devoted to courtesy as opposed to answering the waiting call?*

Job description. After each job has been analyzed, it must be described. If the job is described in terms of its economic value to the employer, then it may have to be redescribed in terms of the human skills and effort required to perform it.

> **Example:** *A security guard's job may be to "check the identification of anyone entering or leaving, allow no wrapped parcels to pass in or out, and generally protect the premises during off-shift hours." The skills to perform that job, however, may begin with proficiency in using firearms, if the guard is to be armed. The effort required may include keeping a rigid checkpoint schedule; or it may involve telling valued customers—tactfully—that they will have to return during normal business hours. These are the factors that the employer will list when it describes the guard job in terms of what it takes to perform it.*

Employee evaluation follows job evaluation. It is only after a job has been described in terms of what is required to perform it that evaluation of those doing the job becomes possible. Analyzing and describing the various jobs within an organization may be extremely difficult and, if there is no foundation, may be a major project.

Take the necessary time to analyze job elements completely before any thought is given to developing a system for evaluating the employees who will perform the jobs.

Once the jobs have been broken into their elements and the skills, abilities and effort needed to perform them have been identified, you can focus on evaluating individual performance. A good evaluation system will enable management to accurately measure the varying results its individual employees achieve in performing their jobs.

Prepare for the appraisal

One way to help ensure your performance appraisals are effective is to coach those conducting the appraisal meeting, usually the immediate supervisor, on how to prepare for the meeting. Don't assume that your managers know what it means to "be prepared;" you need to tell them.

Checklist

Preparing for the appraisal meeting

- ☐ **Be familiar with the employee's job functions.** Decide which functions are the most critical. Define the specific activities and responsibilities that contribute to those functions.
- ☐ **Gather information.** Compare what should have been done with the employee's actual performance. Use notes, production reports, customer or coworker feedback, and any other available records to back up the appraisal.
- ☐ **Identify critical incidents.** Identify situations where the employee has made an outstanding contribution or has experienced a failure when attempting to fulfill an important job function.
- ☐ **Review previous appraisals.** Determine whether the employee has met realistic performance goals set in previous reviews.
- ☐ **Prepare a development plan.** The plan should aim to strengthen conduct that leads to good performance and to change conduct that pulls performance down.
- ☐ **Plan for the appraisal discussion.** Limit the objectives and topics of the discussion. Concentrate on only those elements of performance that are critical, very important, or important. Allow time for the employee to provide a self-assessment. Also allow time for you and the employee to explore the causes of problems, as well as time to set goals and work out a development plan for the next review period.
- ☐ **Choose a time and place for the meeting.** Plan enough time for the meeting. Make sure the meeting does not conflict with either your schedule or the employee's schedule. Give the employee enough time to prepare psychologically for the meeting. Encourage the employee to prepare a self-evaluation prior to the meeting. Choose a place for the meeting where you and the employee will have privacy.

Maintain "need-to-know" basis for access

What should management do with the information it collects through its evaluation system? There is, it turns out, a good deal of debate over how employee evaluations should be used. There has been misuse of information in the past. Safeguards must be incorporated to protect data.

Access to performance appraisal information should be limited to a need-to-know basis.

As with other confidential information belonging to the organization, care should be exercised so that performance appraisals are not left lying around for anyone to see or located in unprotected computer databases. Employees have a right to expect that their privacy will be protected. This can be especially important with a negative performance appraisal because an employee may claim that he or she was defamed by the organization.

Best Practices
Tips for making negative appraisals positive

- Be familiar with the details of the employee's job, workload, working conditions, and resources available.
- Be prepared to describe performance deficiencies objectively, specifically, and honestly.
- View the appraisal meeting not as a punishment, but as a positive tool for helping the employee to improve.
- Don't point fingers at the employee. Focus on the conduct and not the person.
- Emphasize behavior that is desired in the future rather than dwelling on past misconduct.
- Ask questions. Seek the employee's input as to why he or she is performing poorly.
- Be a good listener. Be respectful of the employee's opinions, even if you disagree.

- Develop strategies for improving the poor job performance. Explore with the employee how poor performance can be turned into success.
- Have a positive outlook. Let the employee know that you are confident that he or she can improve.

The Quiz

1. A personnel action such as discipline or discharge generally may be defended from challenge if it is taken pursuant to a legitimate business justification. ❑ True ❑ False

2. Performance appraisal systems fail when they are based on subjective opinions about how a person is performing. ❑ True ❑ False

3. Performance appraisals should never contain more than conclusory statements about an employee's deficiencies or conduct. ❑ True ❑ False

4. What are some of the key elements that supervisors should remember when making performance appraisals?
    a. Document both positive and negative behaviors
    b. Negate employee comments
    c. Give details
    d. Soften a negative appraisal
    e. Review prior appraisals
    f. All of the above
    g. None of the above
    h. A, C, and E
    i. A and D

Continued on next page

Continued from previous page

5. Inaccurate appraisals may result from the appraiser having insufficient information about job performance, or the job itself. ❑ True ❑ False

Answer key: 1. T; 2. T; 3. F; 4. H; 5. T

Chapter 5

Time away from work

Navigating the leave laws 104
Family and medical leave 104
    BEST PRACTICES: What happens
        if leave isn't designated appropriately? 111
Overlapping leave laws:
    ADA, FLMA and workers' compensation 116
    BEST PRACTICES: Coordinating FMLA,
        ADA and workers' compensation policies 120
Pregnancy leave 121
Military leave 123
Other leaves required by law 125
Company-offered leave 125
Be familiar with company policy 126
Avoid disability bias pitfalls 126
The Quiz 128

Grace, an employee in your organization, announced her pregnancy two months ago. Since that time, she has missed 12 days of work due to severe morning sickness. Alec, Grace's supervisor, is very upset by all these absences. As a manager responsible for meeting the unit's business goals, he would never put up with this kind of absence record from a nonpregnant employee. He wants to discipline Grace for her absences. To make matters worse, Grace just told Alec that she's been put on bed rest for 10 days because of a complication in her pregnancy. Alec requested medical certification of the need for rest from Grace's obstetrician.

    Later that same day, Grace's coworker, Leeza, requested sick leave. Her doctor ordered her to stay off her feet for three days, hoping to relieve severe swelling in Leeza's sprained ankle. Alec granted the leave and did not request medical certification. Did Alec do the right thing?

Navigating the leave laws

HR professionals are the "go to" people for managers and supervisors who are confronted with leave requests. While it's likely that a manager or supervisor will be the one who hears an employee say, "I need time off," or "I've been hurt," or "I can't come in today," it is the HR professional who supplies the information necessary for a response. Absences may raise issues under the Family and Medical Leave Act (FMLA), the Americans with Disabilities Act (ADA), and if a workplace injury is involved, state workers' compensation statutes.

Navigating these leave laws can be extremely challenging. Therefore, you need to understand how they intersect so that you can advise the manager or supervisor on what questions to ask and what potentially unlawful questions to avoid.

Where do you start? When confronted by a leave request, start by asking "Is the employee covered?" Since you must analyze each leave request under each law separately, take it one step at a time.

Failing to effectively manage employee leave can result in workflow interruption, financial drain and legal consequences.

Family and medical leave

To determine whether an employee is eligible for leave, the federal Family and Medical Leave Act is a good starting point. The law guarantees an eligible employee up to 12 weeks of job-protected leave each year for any one or more of the following reasons:
- birth of child;
- adoption of child;
- foster care of child;
- child's serious health condition;
- spouse's serious health condition;
- parent's serious health condition;
- employee's serious health condition;
- employee's pregnancy.

FMLA leave for the birth, adoption, or foster care of a child can be taken by men and women. Denying leave to an eligible employee on the basis of gender can result in FMLA and sex discrimination liability.

What conditions are serious?

A serious health condition is an illness, injury, or impairment that involves any of the following:

- ◆ Any period of incapacity connected with inpatient care (overnight stay) in a hospital, hospice, or residential medical care facility.
- ◆ Any period of incapacity requiring absence of more than three days from work, school, or other regular daily activities that also involves continuing treatment by or under the supervision of a health care provider.

- ◆ Continuing treatment by or under the supervision of a health care provider for a chronic or long-term health condition that is incurable or is so serious that, if not treated, would likely result in a period of incapacity for more than three days.
- ◆ Incapacity due to pregnancy or prenatal care.

If an employee is absent for more than three consecutive calendar days—and this can include a weekend—it's important to communicate with the employee in order to determine the reason for the leave.

What conditions are not serious?

The following conditions are generally not considered serious health conditions:

- ◆ Conditions not involving inpatient care or continuing treatment.
- ◆ Unless complications develop, the common cold, flu, ear aches, upset stomach, minor ulcers, headaches other than migraines, routine dental or orthodontia problems, or periodontal disease.
- ◆ Unless inpatient care is required or complications develop, cosmetic treatments (treatments for acne or plastic surgery, for example).
- ◆ Absences because of an employee's use of a substance, rather than for treatment of substance abuse.

FMLA leave in connection with substance abuse may only be taken for treatment of substance abuse.

Are you covered by the law?

Employers in private industry with 50 or more employees are subject to the FMLA. Public agencies, including schools, are also subject to the FMLA regardless of how many employees they employ.

Although all employees are counted for purposes of determining whether an employer employs 50 or more employees, not all of these employees are necessarily eligible for leave benefits.

An employee at a worksite with less than 50 employees is eligible for FMLA leave if the total number of persons employed by the employer within 75 miles of the worksite adds up to 50. The number of employees maintained on your payroll determines how many employees are employed within 75 miles of an employee's worksite.

The determination is made on the date the employee requests leave.

If your company employed 60 people in August when an employee requests leave to be taken in December for elective surgery, but only 40 employees are still employed in December, the leave still must be granted (assuming the other rules are met).

Determine employee's eligibility for leave

Not all employees are entitled to take FMLA leave. An employee's eligibility depends on the number of employees the employer has at a given worksite and the hours the employee has worked. Assuming your organization is covered by the law, you'll need to know:

◆ How long the employee has worked for your organization.
◆ The reason for the requested leave.
◆ The amount of leave the employee has already taken.

Only employees who have worked for the organization for 12 months—they do not have to be 12 consecutive months—and who worked at least 1,250 hours during that 12-month period—are eligible for FMLA leave. Brand-new employees who have never worked for your organization aren't immediately eligible. Part-time and seasonal employees are not eligible if they worked fewer than 1,250 hours in the preceding 12 months.

If you don't have records proving an employee hasn't worked 1,250 hours in the last 12 months, the employee is presumed to qualify.

Right to request additional information

An employee is not required to say the magical words "I need FMLA leave" in order to put the employer on notice that leave requested qualifies under the FMLA. Rather, it is the employer's responsibility to determine whether leave qualifies for FMLA protection based on the information provided by the employee.

FMLA protection begins when an employee asks for time off for a qualifying reason. If the employee does not provide enough information for the employer to determine whether the FMLA applies, additional information should be requested. If the employee fails to explain why leave is required, the request can be denied.

The Americans with Disabilities Act (ADA) limits the type of questions that can be asked of employees. Employers may only make disability-related inquiries (questions likely to elicit information about a disability) if they are *job-related and consistent with business necessity*. Questions regarding the nature, severity, or condition causing the disability are prohibited. Questions that are not likely to elicit information about a disability are permitted as long as they are not phrased in terms of a disability. Employers are permitted to ask employees about their general well-being; whether they can perform their general job functions; and about their current use of illegal drugs.

Employers will not violate the ADA by asking for information specified in the FMLA medical certification form [see, "Right to request medical certification," below]. In order to get the information needed to make a decision as to whether the FMLA applies, employers should ask the employee whether the reason for the request involves a serious health condition.

Notify employees of leave rights

Employers have very specific notice obligations under the law. These obligations are triggered when an employee requests leave.

Employers who have employee handbooks must provide FMLA information in the handbook.

Employers without written policies or handbooks still have to provide written guidance about FMLA rights and obligations but only when FMLA leave is requested. The employer may duplicate and give the employee a copy of the FMLA Fact Sheet issued by the Wage and Hour Division of the Department of Labor.

When employees ask for time off that qualifies as FMLA leave, employers must give them written notice detailing specifically what the employee must do and explaining any consequences of failing to do so. This notice can also serve to acknowledge and document specific requests for leave.

✓ Checklist
Required elements for FMLA notice

Notice must include the following items:
- ☐ That leave will be counted against annual FMLA leave entitlement;
- ☐ Any requirement that an employee furnish medical certification of a serious health condition, and the consequences of failing to furnish medical certification;
- ☐ The employee's right to substitute paid leave, whether the employer will require substitution, and the conditions related to any substitution;
- ☐ Any requirements or arrangements for the employee to make health benefits premium payments;
- ☐ Any requirement that the employee present a fitness-for-duty certificate to be restored to employment;
- ☐ The employee's status as a "key" employee, if applicable;
- ☐ An employee's right to restoration to the same or an equivalent job; and
- ☐ The employee's potential liability for payment of health insurance premiums paid by the employer during the employee's unpaid FMLA leave if the employee fails to return to work.

Maintain control by designating leave quickly

It is important to act quickly to determine whether leave—either requested or in some cases, already taken—qualifies as FMLA leave. Employers must designate leave, at least conditionally and verbally, within two business days after learning of reasons that qualify for FMLA protection. Written notice that the leave will count as FMLA leave must follow no later than the next payroll period.

What are the consequences to the employer for failing to designate a qualifying leave as FMLA leave? Under Department of Labor regulations, employers may not count any absences against an employee's 12-week FMLA leave entitlement if there has been no designation by the employer that leave qualifies as FMLA leave. But the US Supreme Court invalidated this aspect of the regulation, saying that the Labor Department did not have the authority to potentially extend leave entitlement beyond 12 weeks because of a failure to designate it. The decision has been interpreted to mean that failing to strictly comply with some of the more technical aspects of the FMLA won't necessarily make the employer liable unless the employee affected suffers some harm.

Even so, designating qualifying leave as FMLA leave gives employers a way to control their leave policies. An employee who is out on extended sick leave, for example, may come back to work and immediately ask for FMLA leave for another qualifying reason. If the sick leave has not been designated as FMLA leave, the employee conceivably could then be entitled to an additional full 12 weeks for FMLA leave.

When time off from work is an issue, employers need to:
- ask questions about the nature of the leave;
- characterize the employee's leave as FMLA leave, if appropriate;
- inform the employee that the leave has been designated as FMLA leave in a timely fashion; and
- confirm the leave designation in writing if oral notice was given. A notation on the employee's next pay stub is sufficient.

Remember Grace, the pregnant employee who missed 12 days of work due to severe morning sickness? Alec, her manager, should have notified HR immediately after Grace's announcement that one of his staff members was pregnant. Next, Alec should have informed Grace that all future leave days, and partial days, that are pregnancy related would be treated as family medical leave. Alec will also want to make sure that Grace is given the organization's information for pregnant employees. Finally, Alec should document his actions and place them in a confidential file. By taking these actions, Alec can maintain control of his organization's leave policies.

Best Practices

What happens if leave isn't designated appropriately?

As a practical matter, the Supreme Court's decision should not affect, in any significant way, how employers deal with FMLA situations, says management attorney Sue K. Willman. It does, however, give reassurances to employers that technical violations of the FMLA's frequently burdensome and complex regulations will not necessarily impose liability on the employer unless the employee is actually harmed in some way.

Make a good faith effort. Employers still need to make a good faith effort to comply with the FMLA and to minimize potential harm to employees. So why take an unnecessary risk?

Give notice of designation as soon as possible, even if outside the two-day period. Employers should try to follow the regulations as closely as possible, but at a minimum give all notices as soon as reasonably possible, even if it's outside the time periods required by the regulations. "If the designation is made within a reasonable period of time under the circumstances, and the employee will not be harmed, then the employer is probably safe in counting the leave retroactively, even if the regulations technically prohibit retroactive designations," Willman suggests.

Minimize potential harm to employees. An employer should focus more on ensuring reasonable and accurate communications and preventing and minimizing harm to an employee than worrying about technical compliance with the regulations. In all situations, the employer should do whatever would be fair and reasonable to minimize or prevent harm to an employee, Willman urges.

Right to request medical certification

Employees can be required to support requests for medical leave, either for themselves or to care for a family member with a serious health condition, with a certification issued by a health care provider. The employee must provide this certification within 15 calendar days of the request, unless it is not practical to do so under the circumstances.

Employers must advise the employee whether medical certification will be required when the employee requests leave.

Checklist

Information required for medical certification

A certification is considered sufficient if it includes the following information:

- ☐ date on which the serious health condition began;
- ☐ probable duration;
- ☐ appropriate medical facts;
- ☐ estimate of amount of time needed;
- ☐ statement that the eligible employee is needed to care for the family member or that the employee is unable to perform the functions of the employee's position;
- ☐ dates and duration of planned medical treatment for a request for intermittent or reduced schedule leave;
- ☐ medical necessity for leave and duration, in the case of an employee's serious health condition, for a request for intermittent or reduced schedule leave and;
- ☐ necessity of the employee's assistance and duration of leave for a request for intermittent or reduced schedule leave in the case of the serious health condition of an employee's family member.

Chapter 5—Time away from work

> If an employee fails to provide the requested medical certification in a timely manner, an employer may deny FMLA leave until the employee submits the certification.

An employer may also maintain a uniformly applied practice or policy of requiring returning employees to provide certification that they are able to resume work.

Pay during leave

FMLA leave is unpaid. However, companies can require employees to take paid leave they have already earned, such as vacation or sick leave, during FMLA leave. If substitution of paid leave is required, notification to the employee must be made within two business days of the employee's notice of the need for leave, or when a determination is made that the leave is FMLA-qualifying. Generally speaking, the designation must be made before the leave starts, unless there is insufficient information about the employee's reason for taking leave.

Notice of intent to return to work

You have the right to require employees on FMLA leave to report periodically regarding their status and their intent to return to work once their leave expires. Requests for status reports must be reasonable under the particular circumstances of the employee's case. FMLA protections end for employees who say they are definitely not returning to work.

> Be careful: an employee's intention not to return to work must be absolutely clear, certain, and subject to no possible misunderstanding.

Bargaining agreements

Employers must comply with any collective bargaining agreement or employee benefit program that provides greater leave rights. No collective bargaining agreement or employee benefit or plan can diminish the rights established for employees by the FMLA. Unions cannot bargain away employees' FMLA rights.

Reinstating returning employees

Returning employees must be given the same position they held when leave began or a position with equivalent benefits, pay and terms and conditions of employment—even if the employee was replaced or the position was restructured during the employee's absence.

An equivalent position means one that is virtually identical to the employee's former position.

WHAT you need to know

While employers may accommodate an employee's request for a different shift, schedule or position, they cannot require that the employee accept a different position or shift against the employee's wishes.

Prohibited practices

✓ Checklist
Prohibited employer practices under FMLA

An employer may not interfere with, restrain, or deny the exercise of or attempt to exercise, any right provided to employees by the FMLA. Unlawful interference could include:

☐ refusing to authorize an eligible employee to take FMLA leave;
☐ discouraging an eligible employee from using FMLA leave;
☐ manipulating the work force to avoid FMLA responsibilities, such as unnecessarily transferring employees from one work site to another in order to keep work sites below the 50-employee threshold;
☐ failing to provide an employee who is on FMLA leave with the same benefits that are normally provided to an employee on leave without pay;
☐ using the taking of FMLA leave as a negative factor in employment actions, such as promotions or disciplinary actions;
☐ counting FMLA leave under no fault attendance policies; and
☐ inducing an employee to waive his or her FMLA rights.

Let's revisit Alec and Grace. Although Alec was upset by the frequency of Grace's absences, employers cannot discriminate against employees who have used FMLA leave, whether for pregnancy or for other reasons. Consequently, an employee's use of family medical leave may not be considered as a negative factor in disciplinary actions.

Nor can employers count family medical leave absences against the organization's absence policy. Use of family medical leave may not be counted against an organization's "no-fault" attendance policy. As a result, Alec should not discipline Grace for her pregnancy-related absences.

It is also unlawful for an employer to discharge or in any other way discriminate against any individual for opposing any practice that is unlawful under the FMLA.

> You can discharge an employee who is on FMLA leave if you can demonstrate that the employee would not have been employed at the time of termination—for example, terminating an employee on FMLA leave as part of a legitimate reduction in force.

What you don't know can hurt you

When it comes to the FMLA, ignorance is not bliss. Nor is it an excuse for failing to comply with its requirements. What are the consequences if an employer fails to actively comply with the FMLA?

- **Up to 12 weeks of wages.** Remember you cannot interfere with employee rights that are protected by the FMLA—and that means the right to take leave. If an employer violates the law, the affected employee may be entitled to receive wages, salary, benefits, or other compensation lost because of the violation—up to 12 weeks of wages, plus interest.
- **Medical expenses.** If an employer violates the FMLA by failing to maintain an employee's group health benefits during leave, the employer becomes responsible for that employee and has to pay for any medical expenses of the employee that would have been covered by the group health plan.
- **Double damages.** In addition, damages may be doubled unless the employer can prove that it acted in good faith based on a reasonable belief that it wasn't violating the FMLA.

- **Fees and costs.** The employer may also be held responsible for paying the employee's attorney's fees, witness fees, and court costs on top of the damages mentioned above.
- **Equitable relief.** If a court finds that it is appropriate, it can order the employer to give the affected employee a job, reinstate the employee, or even promote the employee.

Not knowing how the FMLA works can be very costly. And it can result in personal liability for corporate officers, including managers, supervisors, and HR professionals who are found to be acting in the interest of the employer.

Overlapping leave laws: ADA, FMLA and workers' compensation

Private employers with 50 or more employees are covered by both the FMLA and the ADA. So are state and local government employers with 15 or more employees. These employers have varying obligations under the two laws that can be overlapping and a source of confusion. In addition, employees who are injured while at work may be entitled to workers' compensation benefits.

If an employee is eligible for leave under more than one of these laws, which kind of leave applies? The distinction is important, because the type of leave determines the rights and obligations of both you and the employee.

If the employee does not specify the type of leave he or she is requesting, you must do what the law requires: Select the kind of leave most favorable to the employee. That will be the leave that allows the employee the greatest amount of time off or allows the employee to retain the most benefits, including pay, during leave.

The FMLA and the ADA both require a covered employer to grant medical leave to an employee in certain circumstances.

Serious health condition v. disability

The FMLA and the ADA may interact when an employee's serious health condition is involved. The illness may allow an employee to qualify for FMLA leave only (tonsillitis, for example) but if it substantially impairs the employee's ability to perform a major life activity (a stroke or heart attack, for example), the employer has a duty to make reasonable accommodations for the employee.

Reasonable accommodation could involve unpaid leave—and this unpaid leave is not limited to 12 weeks.

Under the ADA, a qualified individual with a disability may receive more than 12 weeks of leave as a reasonable accommodation, so long as the leave does not impose an undue hardship on the employer's business. After FMLA leave, an employee can be transferred to an alternative position, so long as it is "equivalent." Under the ADA, an employee returning from a "reasonable accommodation" leave must be returned to the same job unless to do so would work an undue hardship on the employer. Transfer is permitted under the ADA as a reasonable accommodation, but if there are no vacant positions, an employee can be transferred to a lower paying job.

Intermittent or occasional leave

Under the ADA, an employee may work part-time or occasionally take time off as a reasonable accommodation if it doesn't impose an undue hardship on the employer. If reduced hours create an undue hardship in the current position, the employer must see if there is a vacant, equivalent position to which the employee can be reassigned.

Under the FMLA, an eligible employee may take leave intermittently or on a part-time basis for a serious health condition if it is medically necessary for treatment or recovery. This type of leave can last until the employee has used up the equivalent of 12 workweeks in a 12-month period.

Key concepts: ADA v. FMLA

Under the ADA:

An employee who needs leave related to a disability—a substantial impairment to a major life activity—will be entitled to leave if:
- ◆ There is no other effective "reasonable" accommodation, and
- ◆ The leave will not cause undue hardship.

The employee should be allowed to use any accrued paid leave first, but if that is insufficient to cover the entire period, then the employer should grant unpaid leave.

An employer must continue an employee's health insurance benefits during the disability leave period if it does so for other employees in a similar leave status.

The employer must allow a qualified employee to return to the same position—with or without reasonable accommodation—assuming that there was no undue hardship to the employer in holding it open.

If it is an undue hardship for the employee's position to be held open during a period of leave, or an employee is no longer qualified to return to the original position, then the employer must reassign the employee—absent undue hardship—to a vacant position for which the employee is qualified.

Under the FMLA:

An employee is entitled to a maximum of 12 weeks of leave per 12-month period for pregnancy, birth or adoption or a serious health condition of the employee, child or parent.

The employee should be allowed to use any accrued paid leave first, but if that is insufficient to cover the entire period, then the employer should grant unpaid leave.

The employer must continue the employee's health insurance coverage during the leave period, providing the employee pays the employee's share of the premiums.

The FMLA guarantees the right of the employee to return to the same position or to an equivalent one.

The FMLA does not talk about reassignment.

What is workers' compensation?

Workers' compensation is defined by state law and administered by the states. Workers' compensation provides partial income replacement while employees are unable to work and coverage for medical expenses for employees who are temporarily or permanently injured on the job.

> *Unlike employee benefits for disability income and sick pay, workers' compensation payments are made only for on-the-job injuries or occupational illness.*

If an employee is injured on the job or suffers from a work-related illness and is temporarily unable to work, that too is a form of disability leave. The worker gets income replacement benefits while he or she is unable to work and may also be eligible for sick leave—but the combination of workers' compensation benefits and sick leave may not exceed the employee's normal rate of pay.

> Not every workers' compensation injury will result in a disability under the ADA. The key is whether there has been, as a result of the injury, a substantial impairment of a major life activity. If there is, then the employee may be entitled to ADA protection as well.

An employee who is injured or has an accident at the workplace should look to the workers' compensation policy for income and reimbursement of medical expenses. In the case of FMLA, there are many implications for employers trying to coordinate with workers' compensation.

> *Whenever workers' compensation is involved, you should consider ADA and FMLA implications.*

Example: Jesminder is lifting heavy boxes at work, when she feels a sharp pain in her back. She ends up on bed rest. Jesminder qualifies for workers' compensation, and while she is out on leave, she calls you and asks about her FMLA rights. Does the fact that she's absent from work due to a workplace injury preclude her from exercising her FMLA rights?

No. You need to offer the same FMLA protections you would have offered her had she hurt her back in a non-work related incident.

Most state laws allow an employer to end workers' compensation benefits if an employee refuses to take a light-duty job. But be careful! Although an employee may lose workers' compensation benefits, an employer cannot require that an employee return from FMLA leave to a light-duty job.

Best Practices

Coordinating FMLA, ADA and workers' compensation policies

What can you do to effectively manage the confusing requirements of the FMLA, ADA, and your state's workers' compensation statute?

- Make every qualifying absence FMLA leave.
- Designate and provide notice.
- Identify essential functions of all jobs.
- Provide FMLA training.
- Maintain separate confidential records.
- Document all time off from work.
- Establish a reinstatement procedure.
- Establish and enforce a maximum leave of absence.

Taking these actions will limit the potential for having to provide more leave than the law requires.

Make every qualifying absence FMLA leave. Some experts advise employers to count every absence—be it one hour, one day, or one month—as FMLA leave if it qualifies. This has a dramatic impact on how much FMLA time remains to be taken in a solid block. Thus, employers can revise their sick day, personal day, short-term disability, and medical leave policies to provide that leave taken under these policies runs concurrently with the FMLA. This does not happen automatically.

Remember it is a prohibited act under the law to count FMLA absences against a no-fault attendance policy or to deny attendance bonuses based on FMLA absences.

Many states have laws providing some form of family leave. If your state law provides greater benefits than those guaranteed under the federal FMLA, you are required to provide those greater benefits. You are always free to adopt or retain leave policies that are more generous than those required under the FMLA.

Pregnancy leave

The Pregnancy Discrimination Act of 1978 (PDA) is part of Title VII of the Civil Rights Act. It clarifies that the prohibition on sex discrimination extends to discrimination on the basis of pregnancy and childbirth. Depending on the circumstances of a particular pregnancy, the ADA and the FMLA may come into play as well.

Pregnancy-related employment issues can seem intimidating because they potentially involve so many different areas of the law: family leave, disability protections, and sex bias. But when you get right down to it, the law simply requires that you treat pregnant women no worse than similarly situated non-pregnant people—whether they're job applicants or current employees. If you get hung up on the details, try to look at things from that perspective.

Managing pregnant employees is a fact of life for most organizations, so it is important to understand how pregnancy-related absences can be effectively treated under the FMLA. Any period of incapacity, even doctor's visits, due to pregnancy or for prenatal care, is treated under the law as a serious health condition, entitling the pregnant employee to FMLA leave.

Employers can't treat female employees differently because they are pregnant. You may not require a pregnant woman to go on leave at a certain time in her pregnancy unless she is unable to perform the functions of the job. Also, inability to work due to pregnancy must be treated as any other inability to work for a medical reason.

Let's look at Alec and Grace again. Should Alec have required that Grace provide medical certification of her need for bed rest while not requiring Leeza to provide medical certification for the need to rest her badly swollen ankle? Alec needs to make sure he is treating Grace the same way he is treating all other employees who take leave because of a disability.

If Alec does not require medical certification when an employee cannot work because of a medical reason other than pregnancy, it may be viewed as discrimination to require medical certification when the reason for leave is pregnancy-related.

Is pregnancy a "disability" under the ADA? No—pregnancy is not itself considered a "disability." But pregnancy-related ADA claims can arise when there are complications with a pregnancy, or if an employer improperly views a pregnant woman as disabled and discriminates against her on this basis.

If a pregnant employee is temporarily unable to perform her job because of her pregnancy, she must be treated the same as other temporarily disabled employees.

If modified tasks, alternative assignments, available "light" work, or disability leave with pay are provided to other employees with a temporary disability, these all must be provided to the pregnant employee as well.

Military leave

Reservists and members of the National Guard now make up nearly 50 percent of the country's total available military manpower. In the past, two weeks a year and some weekends would be the extent of workplace disruption that employers of reservists and National Guard members would face. Today, however, employees who are called up may be away from their jobs for an extended period while serving on military duty.

Employees are entitled, under the Uniformed Services Employment and Reemployment Rights Act (USERRA) to take leave for military service if the following criteria are met:

- The employee or an appropriate military officer provides advance oral or written notice of military service unless it would be impossible or unreasonable because of military necessity or other reasons.
- The combined length of the employee's prior military absences from the company does not exceed five years.

USERRA applies to all civilian employers regardless of size.

An eligible employee's leave request must be granted. Even if a manager or supervisor finds the timing, duration, frequency, or nature of an eligible employee's military service to be unreasonable, the employee cannot be denied leave from work.

The federal military leave law does not require pay during military leave. However, some companies voluntarily pay reservists the difference between their regular wage and the military pay received during annual summer training.

Employees on military leave have the right to use any accrued vacation or similar leave with pay during military service. However, employers cannot require employees to do so.

The law prohibits employment discrimination because of past, current, or future military obligations. An employee is protected from service-connected discrimination under USERRA if the employee:
- served in the past in a uniformed service and was separated from such service under honorable conditions;
- currently is a member of or is currently serving in a uniformed service;
- has an obligation to serve in a uniformed service; or
- is an applicant for membership in the uniformed service.

Under USERRA, you must count the months and hours that reservists or Guard personnel would have worked if they had not been called up for military service toward their 12-month/1,250 hour FMLA service requirement.

Reemployment obligations

Generally, an employee must be rehired after military service if the employee provided advance oral or written notice (unless doing so would have been impossible or unreasonable); the person did not exceed the five-years service limit; and the person timely reported to work or applied for reemployment.

Resigning from a job in order to enter military service does not cut off an employee's reemployment rights. As long as the employee meets the eligibility requirements, he or she must be reemployed. The employee may lose entitlement to certain job benefits during military service if the employee voluntarily gives written notice of an intent not to return to work after military service. But such a notice will not deprive the employee of reemployment rights and benefits when the employee returns from military service.

Generally, an employee returning from military service must be placed in the job the employee would have held if the employee remained continuously employed, or, if the employee is unqualified or cannot become qualified for that job, in the employee's pre-service job. If the employee cannot be trained to perform either of those jobs, the employee must be placed in any other job that the employee can perform.

Reasonable accommodation must be provided to employees with service-connected disabilities.

Other leaves required by law

Jury duty leave. Federal law gives employees the right to take time off to serve as jurors in federal courts. State laws give employees the right to serve on state and local juries.

Witness duty leave. A number of states have laws permitting employees to serve as witnesses in court.

Time off to vote. State laws generally have laws permitting employees at least two hours of time off to vote.

Time of for school functions. Several states have laws requiring employers to give employees time off to attend certain functions at their children's schools.

Bone marrow or organ marrow donation. Some states require employers to grant employee requests for time off to donate bone marrow or organs.

Company-offered leave

Companies often make available to employees various types of leave that are not required by law, including:
- vacations;
- scheduled holidays;
- "floating" personal holidays;
- bereavement leave;
- marriage leave;
- educational leave;
- sabbaticals;
- sick leave;
- short-term disability;
- long-term disability.

Moreover, some organizations may "add on" to a leave-of-absence law by providing for even more rights than the law requires. For example, company policy may allow a longer period of family and medical leave than is required by law. Or a company may voluntarily choose to pay employees for certain military-related absences.

Be familiar with company policy

Failure to observe employees' rights under company policy can result in lawsuits. Specifically, HR should ensure that managers and supervisors at least know:

- The types of leave available under company policy.
- Leave documentation requirements.
- Which types of leave accrue and carry over into the next year.
- Who is eligible for each type of leave.
- Whether proof of a need to take leave is required.
- Employee notice requirements.
- Employer notice requirements.
- How much leave may be taken.
- Whether pay will continue during leave.
- Types of leave that run concurrently.
- Impact on seniority.
- The position to which a returning employees is entitled.
- Consequences of failure to return to work on time.

Avoid disability bias pitfalls

Leave as an accommodation. If an employee who requests medically related time off from work is not entitled to FMLA leave, workers' compensation leave, or leave under company policy, do not automatically deny leave. Consider whether the person is a "qualified individual with a disability" under the ADA for whom the requested absence may be a reasonable accommodation.

Extension of leave. If an employee's medically related absence continues beyond the amount of leave permitted under the FMLA, workers' compensation, or company policy, do not automatically take action to terminate the employee. Consider whether the person is a "qualified individual with a disability" for whom extension of leave may be a reasonable accommodation.

Reinstatement after accommodation leave. If a "qualified employee with a disability" is provided leave as a reasonable accommodation, the employee must be placed in the same job upon returning to work, unless doing so would impose an undue hardship on the company.

Accommodation upon return. If an employee is unable to perform his or her former job after returning from a medically related absence, do not automatically demote or terminate the employee. Consider whether the employee is a "qualified individual with a disability" who can be reasonably accommodated to perform that job.

If accommodation is not possible in the employee's former job, determine whether a vacant, equivalent position is available that the employee can perform, with or without reasonable accommodation.

Medical information relating to employees or their family members that often is obtained during the course of a medical leave, whether FMLA, ADA, or workers' compensation-related, must be kept in separate, confidential files.

DON'T miss this

The Quiz

1. An employee must specifically state that he or she needs FMLA leave in order to put the employer on notice that the requested leave qualifies under the FMLA.   ❑ True   ❑ False

2. If an employee fails to provide requested medical certification in a timely manner, an employer may deny FMLA leave until the employee submits certification.   ❑ True   ❑ False

3. Pregnancy is considered a disability under the ADA.   ❑ True   ❑ False

4. USERRA applies to all civilian employers regardless of size.   ❑ True   ❑ False

5. Under USERRA, you must count the months and hours that reservists or National Guard personnel would have worked if they had not been called up for military service toward their 12-month/ 1,250 hour FMLA service requirement.   ❑ True   ❑ False

Answer key: 1. F; 2. T; 3. F; 4. T; 5. T

Chapter 6

Discrimination

What is discrimination? **130**
Federal law prohibits the following types of discrimination **134**
Effects of past discrimination **148**
State laws **149**
The Quiz **151**

> *Carolina was promoted to department manager six months ago. There've been grumblings about her management style but nothing definite until two longtime employees abruptly resigned on the same day. An evaluation of her department found low morale and slipping productivity, and the evaluator concluded that Carolina was not meeting performance expectations. She was reassigned to a staff position with no cut in salary or grade level. Now Carolina's filed a complaint claiming she was removed from her management position because of discrimination. She was the only Cuban and the only woman running a department.*

What is discrimination?

Job discrimination exists when employees or applicants who are members of a protected group are treated less favorably than others. Antidiscrimination laws require that all persons be given an equal opportunity for employment.

Discrimination is all about making employment decisions based on factors that have nothing to do with a person's ability to do the job.

Protected groups

When reading about discrimination laws, you will frequently see the term "protected group." When the first federal antidiscrimination law was enacted, employment discrimination was widely practiced against specific racial, ethnic and religious minorities and also against women.

But the term "protected group" can apply to whites as well as blacks and to men as well as women, depending on the circumstances. In one instance the protected group may be Muslims, and in another it may be agnostics or atheists.

An accurate definition of "protected group" recognizes this shifting meaning, which requires that whatever group is designated as "protected" is defined, at least in part, by personal characteristics about which discrimination is not allowed.

What personal characteristics are protected? The law protects individuals in their right to take, hold, and advance in a job free of discrimination based on personal characteristics, including: race, ethnicity, religion, sex, national origin, citizenship, age, disability, military service.

Intentional discrimination

Frequently referred to by lawyers as "disparate treatment," intentional discrimination results when an employer consciously bases an employment decision on a person's protected status. An employer intentionally discriminates when it means to do what it does. For example, hiring a less-qualified nonminority individual after more qualified minority persons were rejected would amount to overt bias.

> **Example 1:** Three individuals apply for a technical services position in your organization. Chuanxu and Lin Mei have the certification you're looking for, plus relevant experience. Mike has only recently received his certification. Nonetheless, you hire Mike. Hiring a less-qualified nonminority individual after more qualified minority persons were rejected would amount to intentional discrimination.
>
> **Example 2:** Terminating a White forklift driver for theft of merchandise from the warehouse while retaining a Black forklift driver who had committed the same offense would be intentional discrimination.
>
> **Example 3:** Mel manages a discount store. He does not believe he has any prejudice against men or women. He does believe, however, that men are better suited to work in the sporting goods department as "guys are really into sports and can sell better." On the other hand, Mel believes women are more likely to rack up sales in the housewares department. When he looking to fill a position in sporting goods, Mel looks for a man. The same is true for women and the housewares department. Mel's behavior amounts to intentional discrimination.

If you become aware of practices that result in forbidden discrimination, you have an affirmative duty to see that the practice is corrected. Passively accepting or agreeing to unlawful discrimination by another person constitutes forbidden discrimination on the part of the observer.

If an employee or applicant claims to have suffered from disparate treatment, an employer can not use "business necessity" as a defense (see the discussion under "Unintentional discrimination," below). The business necessity defense does not apply to intentional discrimination claims.

To avoid charges of intentional discrimination:
- Use only job-related factors as the basis for employment decisions—whether decisions about hiring, transfers, promotions, discipline, layoffs, terminations, pay or job environment.
- Never base an employment decision on a person's membership in a protected group.
- Treat all employees consistently and fairly.

Unintentional discrimination

Discrimination need not be intentional in order to be unlawful. Any employment practice that's shown to have the effect of screening out members of a protected group at a disproportionately higher rate than persons not belonging to the group can be discriminatory. This type of unintentional discrimination is also known as disparate impact discrimination. The unlawful employment practice can be a current method of doing business or a system that, although unbiased on its face, perpetuates past discrimination.

> **Example:** *Clear-Sky Windows is a window cleaning service specializing in skyscrapers. It requires its window washers to have a high school diploma. But having a diploma has nothing to do with the ability to wash windows, which is the only duty of the job. If members of a certain race or sex in the community where the service operates are less likely to have a diploma, the requirement may be said to have a disparate impact on members of that race or sex.*

An employment practice that has a disparate impact on a protected group can be defended by a showing that the practice is justified by business necessity. However, even if business necessity justifies the practice, the practice will be held unlawful if a less discriminatory alternative method is available that would serve an employer's business needs but is rejected.

> "Business necessity" must be related to job performance or to accurately measuring the capability to perform the job, plus there must be no nondiscriminatory practice that would be equally effective to meet the employer's needs. The business necessity exception has been linked primarily to safety or efficiency considerations. *Business convenience* is not enough.

Safety and efficiency are two types of job-related concerns that can form the basis of a business necessity claim. However, these factors alone are not enough without a showing that there is no acceptable alternative practice that would accomplish the same objective as well. Consider the following examples:

> **Example 1: Public safety.** *Because of the high degree of economic and human risk involved, an airline was justified in requiring flight experience plus a college degree as job qualifications for a pilot's position, notwithstanding the racially discriminatory impact of that policy.*
>
> **Example 2: Safety and efficiency.** *A construction company supervisor's selection of only individuals he knew as the most experienced and qualified to install fire brick in blast furnaces was justified in order to assure the installation was done on time and the safety hazards and extra costs resulting from improper work were avoided.*
>
> **Example 3: Neither safety nor efficiency.** *The desire to cater to alleged customer preference, like a restaurant's belief that customers prefer male to female wait staff, is not a valid "business necessity" defense.*

HR How-to: EMPLOYMENT LAW

✓ Checklist

Key federal antidiscrimination laws that every HR person should know:

- ☐ **Title VII of the Civil Rights Act of 1964 (Title VII).** Title VII prohibits discrimination on the basis of race, sex, color, religion or national origin.
- ☐ **Age Discrimination in Employment Act of 1967 (ADEA).** The ADEA bans discrimination on the basis of age against persons who are 40 or older.
- ☐ **Americans with Disabilities Act of 1990 (ADA).** The ADA forbids discrimination against qualified individuals with disabilities. The ADA also requires that reasonable accommodations be made to the known physical or mental limitations of qualified applicants or employees.
- ☐ **Equal Pay Act of 1963 (EPA).** Paying workers of one sex at a rate different from that paid to the other sex violates the EPA when jobs involve equal skill, effort, and responsibility *and* are performed under similar working conditions in the same establishment.
- ☐ **Immigration Reform and Control Act of 1986 (IRCA).** IRCA prohibits discrimination on the basis of citizenship against persons who have a legal right to work in this country. IRCA also requires employers to verify that all new hires are authorized to work in the United States.
- ☐ **Uniformed Services Employment and Reemployment Rights Act of 1994 (USERRA).** USERRA bans discrimination on the basis of past, current, or future military service. It also provides for military leaves of absence and reemployment of employees after military leave.

Federal law prohibits the following types of discrimination

Racial discrimination. The ban on racial discrimination is generally considered applicable to members of racial minorities. Racial discrimination is when a person's race is used as the reason for the way they are treated.

Race generally refers to classifications based on descendents of the original peoples of varous geographical areas.

Example 1: *The only Black employee in the department works in a room with racist graffiti on the walls and work surfaces. Despite his complaint, nothing is done to clean up the graffiti or said to other employees to discourage new graffiti from being written. This is racial harassment.*

Example 2: *A Hispanic employee who was passed over for a position and salary upgrade for the second time has been subjected to disparaging and racially insensitive comments after asking her boss a year ago what she could do to improve her chances of being promoted into a management position. This is racial discrimination.*

Interracial marriage protected. The ban on race discrimination has been liberally construed to cover adverse employment actions taken against an individual because the individual was involved in an interracial marriage.

Color discrimination. Discrimination because of color would seem inapplicable in most cases; the color of a person's skin would usually classify him or her as a member of a particular race. However, any discrimination against a person with a skin color other than that of the majority in the particular job situation could be used as a basis for asserting discrimination claims.

Whether discrimination is on the basis of race or color is a potentially difficult question, but it rarely is an issue—when an individual can be readily identified as belonging to a minority classification, there is no need for anthropological distinctions on race and color.

Color discrimination can appear when the skin coloring of the members of a particular race varies.

> **Example:** *A light-skinned Black supervisor makes numerous derogatory comments, is antagonistic and cursorily trains a dark-skinned Black employee. This could be evidence of discrimination on the basis of color.*

National origin discrimination. National origin discrimination occurs when an employment decision is based on an individual's national origin, for example, refusing to consider for hire or promotion individuals of Middle Eastern appearance or descent.

> **Example:** *Hiring a White woman without the desired education or experience and refusing to hire an Indian woman who repeatedly applied for an open position and had the required levels of relevant experience and education could be discrimination on the basis of national origin.*

Basing an employment decision on an applicant's or employee's lack of English language skills is also illegal and can be considered national origin discrimination when a language requirement has nothing to do with the ability to successfully perform the job. However, language requirements are allowed if they can be shown to be job-related.

English-only rules. Refusing to allow employees of foreign descent to use their familiar language during either working or nonworking time is discriminatory if there is no sound business considerations for having such a policy.

Example 1: Firing a Parisian employee for speaking French to another Parisian employee at Chicago work site is illegal if speaking French does not prevent the employees from successfully doing their jobs.

Example 2: Firing six employees for refusing to sign a memo detailing an English-only policy which required employees to speak English at all times, including on breaks and when making personal phone calls, would likely be illegal unless it could be shown that such a policy was job-related and consistent with business necessity.

To keep a workplace free of national origin discrimination, an employer must: (1) refrain from ridiculing or harassing an employee because of their national origin and (2) not tolerate such conduct from other employees.

Sex discrimination. Making an employment decision based upon a person's sex constitutes sex discrimination. Remember Carolina and her claim that she was removed from her manager's position because she was the only woman running a department? As an HR professional, you will want to be able to substantiate that the decision to reassign Carolina was not based upon her sex but upon her poor performance as a department manager and that any poor manager either has been or would be treated in a similar manner.

Although most complaints are filed by women, the law prohibiting sex discrimination applies to both men and women. Any criteria an employer uses to make a decision that has an adverse impact on one sex or the other must be job-related.

> **Example 1:** *Firing a male employee, who had no performance problems, after he returned late from lunch for the third day in a row, but not firing the female employee who had multiple performance problems when she also returned late from lunch for the third day in a row, might constitute discrimination on the basis of sex.*
>
> **Example 2:** *A female manager with an advanced degree and five years in-house experience is paid less than a newly hired male manager with a college degree and no management experience. Without more evidence to justify the wage disparity, this is likely unlawful sex discrimination.*

DON'T miss this

Sex is a category, like race, that calls for affirmative action when there is an underutilization in certain jobs measured by availability.

Pregnancy discrimination. Employers are not allowed to make decisions that discriminate against women because of pregnancy, childbirth or related medical conditions. The ban on pregnancy discrimination covers all areas of employment including hiring, promotion, seniority rights and fringe benefits. Examples of pregnancy discrimination include the following:

> **Example 1:** *A sales representative with a good performance record was excluded from all sales meetings, demoted and subjected to overt hostility by her supervisor after becoming pregnant.*
>
> **Example 2:** *A male department manager told his newly hired secretary, while handing her the classified section, that he had never worked with a pregnant woman and wasn't about to start now, so she needed to look for another job.*

Chapter 6—Discrimination

Worst case scenario

Gillian, a part-time bank teller, is expected to be available to substitute for absent full-time bank tellers, particularly during the summer vacation months. After learning she was pregnant and that her baby was due in August, Gillian told her supervisor, Steve of her pregnancy and her decision to work until she delivered. Steve, a bank vice-president, immediately fired Gillian, telling her that she was being dismissed because her pregnancy would require special treatment and that she would be unavailable to fulfill her job responsibility of substituting for absent full-time tellers.

During court proceedings, the bank did not dispute that Gillian was fired because she was pregnant and argued to the court that it was impossible to separate her job performance from her medical condition. Her pregnancy would make her unavailable to fulfill her job responsibilities, namely substituting for vacationing full-time tellers. The court rejected the bank's arguments and found the bank had discriminated against Gillian because of her pregnancy.

Did the bank had a good faith basis to believe that Gillian would be unavailable during the summer to fulfill her employer's legitimate job expectations? Probably not. Steve and Gillian's discussion about her ability to work through her pregnancy was brief and occurred only after Steve announced her dismissal. Gillian did not ask for special treatment or leave and had actually said she planned on working until she delivered.

Assuming summer availability was a bona fide occupational qualification, there was nothing to support the bank's belief that Gillian would be unable to fulfill the bank's job expectations. Gillian did not have an attendance problem, did not request leave and, in fact, announced that she planned to work until she delivered. Steve merely "anticipated" that Gillian's pregnancy would necessitate her unavailability. The bank could not fire Gillian simply because it "anticipated" that she would be unable to fulfill its job expectations.

Sexual harassment. Employers have an obligation to prevent the harassment of employees. According to the Equal Employment Opportunity Commission Guidelines, sexual harassment consists of unwelcome sexual advances, requests for sexual favors, or any other verbal or physical conduct of a sexual nature. An employer acts illegally when it allows sexually offensive, intimidating or hostile conduct to interfere with an individual's work performance.

Any unwanted and abusive conduct directed toward one gender in the workplace can be sexual harassment.

Sexual conduct can create a hostile environment if it unreasonably interferes with an employee's work performance or creates a negative work environment.

> **Example:** *A supervisor's daily, explicit comments and questions to a nurse about her personal life and sexual activity in front of coworkers and patients, such as that she must really enjoy sex since she has several children and whether she had taken men home or "got any," on a continuing basis, created a hostile work environment.*

Nonsexual gender-based conduct can also create a hostile environment. Unwelcome verbal or physical conduct that is hostile or denigrates an employee because of that employee's gender can be the basis for a sexual harassment claim.

> **Example:** *Adriana worked as the first woman salesperson for a car dealership. Her male coworkers responded to her presence with a steady stream of vulgar and offensive gender-based comments, including name-calling, pictures, and notes, where she was called "whore," "bitch" and other words degrading to women.*

✓ Checklist

Examples of gender harassment

According to the EEOC, nonsexual conduct that may be the basis of unlawful gender-based discrimination when based on the gender of the person subjected to it includes:

- ☐ offensive language, including vulgar or profane language;
- ☐ physical conduct, such as obstructing one's path or pushing;
- ☐ berating an individual for mistakes;
- ☐ criticizing work performance;
- ☐ strict enforcement of absence or tardiness rules;
- ☐ removing duties or responsibilities;
- ☐ additional work;
- ☐ forbidding conversation with coworkers;
- ☐ refusal to instruct; and
- ☐ failure to cooperate.

Like other forms of workplace harassment, sexual harassment is viewed by the perception of the victim. In other words, sexual or gender-based conduct in the workplace is unwelcome when an employee does not solicit or initiate the conduct and when the employee reasonably regards the conduct as undesirable and offensive. It does not matter whether the person engaging in the conduct would consider the behavior offensive. All that matters is whether the individual on the receiving end reasonably finds it offensive.

Sexual harassment can involve the transposition of roles or involve individuals of the same sex. The only issue is whether the harasser is treating the victim a particular way because of his or her gender. An employer might even be liable for the harassing conduct of persons outside its employment, such as customers or vendors.

Although the most common occurrence of sexual harassment is between a male supervisor and a female subordinate, sexual harassment can also occur between a female supervisor and a male subordinate or between individuals of the same sex.

> ***Example:*** *Male employees who grope, make derogatory and sexually explicit remarks, and threaten to rape a male coworker have engaged in unlawful sexual harassment.*

Sexual orientation. At this time, discriminating against an individual because of his or her sexual orientation is not prohibited by federal statute. However, the United States Supreme Court's decision striking down state laws against consensual homosexual acts based on constitutionally implied privacy rights bolsters employees' potential legal rights against sexual orientation discrimination.

> *Even though federal statute does not prohibit sexual orientation discrimination, some states and local governments have passed legislation making discrimination on the basis of sexual orientation illegal. Even if an employer is not subject to state or local law banning sexual orientation harassment, an organization is free to set higher standards of conduct by prohibiting it in its workplace.*

Reverse discrimination. Although the basic concern of employment discrimination laws is with women and members of racial and ethnic groups, the protections afforded by federal antidiscrimination laws are not limited to members of any particular race or to one sex.

> ***Example :*** *Selecting a Hispanic employee with no management experience and a "meets expectations" performance evaluation for a management position instead of a White employee with in-plant management experience, an engineering degree and a "superior" performance evaluation may be interpreted as reverse discrimination.*

Religious discrimination. An individual's religious beliefs or practices may not lawfully be given any consideration when making a decision that involves employment opportunities. Religion is defined as including all aspects of religious observances and practice, as well as belief. An employer must decide whether the beliefs professed by an individual are *sincerely held* and whether they are in the individual's own scheme of things religious.

The rule on religious discrimination goes further than requiring an employer to be neutral regarding employee beliefs. An employer must make reasonable efforts to accommodate the religious needs of employees and job applicants.

Even if an employee's religious belief seems incomprehensible or arguably offensive, it is not removed from the protected realm of religious faith. Also, an employee's belief does not have to be held universally within the same sect to be protected.

Example: *A highly qualified associate professor, an Orthodox Jew, informed her department's chairman that she would not be able to teach on Jewish holidays. The chairman suggested she work out a schedule with her students, which she did, and the days she missed because of Jewish holidays were not counted as sick days. However, the professor was unlawfully fired after being repeatedly criticized by her superiors for being unavailable on the Sabbath and for missing department meetings which were scheduled on Jewish holidays despite her attempts to have the meetings rescheduled.*

Age discrimination. Discriminating against persons who are aged 40 years or older is prohibited. However, there are instances when business necessity may justify denying certain job opportunities to persons over the age of 40. Age may be a necessary occupational qualification in the normal operation of a business because of physical degeneration factors.

> **Example:** *Federal courts have continually allowed the Federal Aviation Administration to enforce its "Age Sixty Rule," which limits the age past which individuals can pilot certain aircraft.*

> *Be aware that unlawful discrimination may occur when persons within the protected age range are treated differently. If your department has fourteen employees who are all over the age of 40, treating an employee who is 45 years old differently from the other employees who are between 55 and 60 years old may be interpreted as age discrimination.*

Can employees be forced to retire because of their age? Generally, employees cannot be forced to retire because of their age if they are otherwise capable of performing the duties of their jobs. But an exception is allowed for highly paid executives and top policy makers who are 65 and stand to receive at least $44,000 annually in pension payments. Public safety officers employed by state or local governments can be required to retire pursuant to state law under certain circumstances.

Citizenship discrimination. It is unlawful to discriminate on the basis of citizenship against certain protected individuals, including citizens or nationals of the United States, lawful permanent residents, temporary residents and persons who have been granted refugee or asylum status. If a person does not have lawful status, he or she is not protected from citizenship discrimination.

> **Example:** *An employer's insistence that all Puerto Rican applicants possess green cards even after learning green cards were not required for individuals who were U.S. citizens was found to have discriminated against the applicants on the basis of citizenship.*

The ban on citizenship discrimination does not apply to all terms and conditions of employment. It is only concerned with decisions that involve hiring, recruitment or job referrals where a fee is involved, and terminations.

An employer can avoid citizenship discrimination by checking documents provided by job applicants and attesting to their employability. Be sure you check the identity and eligibility for employment for each applicant, not just those who might be alien. An employer acts illegally if it turns away individuals simply because they appear to be alien or because they lack citizenship status.

Exceptions. Exceptions are allowed in instances where citizenship is made a requirement for employment by federal, state or local government contract or is otherwise required by law. Citizenship status also may be a basis for extending preference to one applicant over another who is an alien. However, the preference is limited to instances where the two individuals are **equally qualified**. The preference goes to any citizen or national of the United States.

Disability discrimination. Employers are prohibited from discriminating against any disabled person who is a "qualified individual with a disability." Two requirements must be met before a person is protected from disability bias: (1) the person must have a disability; and (2) the person must be qualified for the job.

WHAT you need to know

> A person has a disability if the person falls into *any* of the following three categories:
>
> 1. The person has a physical or mental impairment that significantly restricts one or more of the person's major life activities. "Major life activities" are activities that an average person can perform with little or no difficulty such as walking, seeing, hearing, breathing, speaking, learning, performing manual tasks, caring for oneself, or participating in community activities.
> 2. The person does not currently have such an impairment but has a record of such an impairment.
> 3. The person has no such impairment but is regarded by management as having such an impairment.

DON'T miss this

> An individual with a disability is "qualified" for a job if the person meets **both** of the following requirements:
>
> 1. The person meets the necessary requirements for the job, such as experience, education, training, skills, and licenses.
>
> 2. The person can perform the key duties of the job either with or without a reasonable accommodation of the person's disability.

Persons who have a relationship or association with a person with a disability are also protected from discrimination on the basis of that relationship or association.

> **Example:** *It is illegal to refuse to hire a qualified job applicant on the grounds that the applicant does volunteer work helping people with AIDS.*

Reasonable accommodation. Employers have a duty to provide reasonable accommodations to the known physical or mental limitations of a qualified person with a disability. A reasonable accommodation is a change to the way things are usually done that enables such a person to perform the key functions of a job or to enjoy the same benefits and privileges that are available to nondisabled persons.

Chapter 6—Discrimination **147**

Reasonable accommodations must be made only to the *known* physical or mental limitations of persons with disabilities. Generally, an accommodation request from an employee or applicant triggers the duty to accommodate. However, if an employee with a known disability is not performing well, the supervisor may ask the employee if an accommodation is needed.

Accommodations that would impose an undue hardship on the employer's business are not required. An undue hardship occurs if providing the accommodation would be too costly, extensive, disruptive, or would alter the nature or the operation of the business. However, even if providing a particular accommodation would impose an undue hardship, other accommodations must still be considered.

✓ Checklist

Finding a reasonable accommodation

☐ Look at the particular job and determine its purpose and key functions.

☐ Consult with the person with a disability to find out of the precise job-related limitations imposed by the person's disability.

☐ In consultation with the person, identify possible accommodations and assess how effective each accommodation would be in enabling the person to perform key job functions.

☐ If there are several possible accommodations, consider the person's preference and select the accommodation that best serves the needs of the person and the company.

☐ Notify the company official responsible for approving accommodations of (1) the accommodation chosen; and (2) other accommodations to consider if that accommodation is rejected because of undue hardship.

Veterans and military personnel

Employers are prohibited by both federal and state laws from discriminating against those with past, current or future military obligations. The ban is broad and extends to hiring; promotion; reemployment after military service; termination; and any benefit of employment. Anyone who is a past member, current member, or applicant to be a member of the uniformed services is protected from service-connected discrimination.

> **Example 1:** *Forbidding a fire marshal from taking a makeup promotional exam when he missed the first exam due to being on active military duty is unlawful.*
>
> **Example 2:** *Refusing to hire a well-qualified female applicant because she is a member of the Army reserves is prohibited.*
>
> **Example 3:** *Firing an employee the same day he tells you he plans on enlisting in the Marines in the near future is also unlawful.*

Effects of past discrimination

Except for seniority systems, neutral employment practices violate the antidiscrimination laws if they favor white employees over minority workers. Job practices, which appear to operate fairly and in a neutral manner, are unlawful if they perpetuate past discrimination. Even good faith efforts to eliminate all present discrimination do not relieve a party from responsibility for the continuing effects of past bias.

Past discrimination may continue under good faith seniority systems that require employees give up seniority in transferring from one line of job progression to another since federal law has immunized seniority systems from the ban on discrimination.

State laws

Twenty-three-year-old Juan was recruited by your company to fill a management position at one of your satellite offices. One week after beginning work, he met the company president just before a meeting. Looking shocked after the introduction, the president told Juan that he was "too young" to be the vice-president of operations and that it would be embarrassing if anyone outside the company found out his age, position, and salary. Two days later, the president called Juan and told him things weren't working out and asked him to resign. Juan refused, saying he hadn't had a chance to prove himself. He was demoted the next day. Juan has filed an age discrimination complaint under state law but you don't have to worry, right? He's too young to complain about age discrimination.

States have enacted their own fair employment practices legislation. Many state fair employment practices statutes parallel the federal antibias laws. Nevertheless, states are generally free to enact laws that provide greater rights than the federal laws. Thus, types of discrimination not banned by the federal laws can be prohibited by state legislation.

A state law might forbid discrimination because of arrest record, marital status, sexual orientation, breastfeeding, genetic testing, weight, or parenthood, among other protected categories.

DON'T miss this

State legislation can provide wider coverage than the federal laws. For instance, a business employing 10 employees would not covered by Title VII of the 1964 Civil Rights Act but, that same business might still be subject to a state law that contains the same prohibitions as Title VII. State antidiscrimination laws can also mandate further requirements and greater remedies, such as uncapped compensatory and punitive damages.

Some states vary the requirements for status in belonging to a protected group. Remember Juan and his age discrimination complaint? While Juan may not belong to a protected group under federal law, he may belong to a protected group under state law and, therefore, be able to file an age discrimination lawsuit against his employer.

State statutes are superseded by the federal antibias laws to the extent they are inconsistent with the federal laws. For example, so-called state protective laws that limit women's work hours conflict with Title VII's ban on employment discrimination.

In some cases, severe discriminatory conduct could lead to a lawsuit based on state court-created law, such as a claim for intentional infliction of emotional distress. Lawyers often challenge severe discriminatory conduct under both federal and state laws and civil wrong theories in order to maximize the recovery for employees.

Be aware that some municipalities have passed local laws prohibiting conduct that may not be covered by federal or state law. For example, sexual orientation is not prohibited by federal statute but several states and municipalities have enacted laws or ordinances prohibiting discrimination on the basis of a person's sexual orientation.

The Quiz

1. There are no limits to what an employer must do to accommodate a disabled employee. ❏ True ❏ False

2. It's ok to prevent employees from speaking to each other in another language while working because you feel uncomfortable when you don't understand what they're talking about. ❏ True ❏ False

3. Federal and state law bans sexual orientation discrimination. ❏ True ❏ False

4. A state can enact legislation prohibiting discrimination on the basis of a person's marital status ❏ True ❏ False

5. Treating all employees consistently and fairly is a good way to avoid charges of intentional discrimination ❏ True ❏ False

Answer key: 1. F; 2. F; 3. F; 4. T; 5. T

Chapter 7

Harassment

What is harassment? **154**
What is a hostile work environment? **154**
Harassment can be verbal, written, or physical **155**
Types of harassment **157**
Harassers can be coworkers, supervisors or outsiders **159**
Rude conduct isn't necessarily harassment **161**
What if nobody complained? **162**
How can an employer protect itself? **162**
    BEST PRACTICES: Ensuring a thorough investigation **166**
Be discreet **168**
The Quiz **168**

> *Amy's found crying in the ladies' restroom. While a coworker comforts her, Amy blurts out she's being harassed by her supervisor, Frank. Frank has been using vulgar language when talking to her and has asked her several times to have sex with him. He's also been sending daily emails, asking her for a date. She's hiding in the restroom because he tried to grab her as she walked by. Amy doesn't know what to do.*

What is harassment?

Harassment consists of any conduct, verbal or physical, that degrades or shows hostility to another person because of age, disability, gender, national origin, race, religion, veteran status, or any other category protected by law. To be considered illegal harassment, the conduct must create a hostile working environment.

Employers have a responsibility to keep their workplace free from harassment. Although an employer cannot be held responsible for the prejudices of its workers or clientele, it is under a legal duty to take reasonable measures to control or eliminate harassing behavior that expresses those prejudices in the workplace.

This duty to prevent harassment extends not only to workers who are the objects of unlawful harassment, but also to those workers who are offended by the harassment of others.

What is a hostile environment?

A hostile environment exists when:
- an employee has been subjected to verbal or physical conduct that shows hostility toward the employee because of a protected characteristic; and
- the conduct has the purpose or effect of interfering with the employee's work performance or opportunities, or creating an intimidating, hostile or offensive work environment.

Unfortunately, there is no precise test to determine whether conduct based on a protected characteristic has created a hostile environment. There are a couple of "tests" that courts use, however:
- a subjective test, which asks whether the harassment victim actually perceived the conduct to have created a hostile or abusive working environment, and
- an objective test, which asks whether the victim's subjective perception is "reasonable."

To determine whether harassing conduct creates a hostile environment, consider:

- the nature of the conduct (physical, verbal, or both);
- the identity of the harasser (was it a supervisor? coworker? non-employee?);
- whether the conduct was physically threatening or merely an offensive comment;
- how frequent, pervasive, or severe the conduct was;
- the context in which the conduct occurred;
- whether the conduct was unwelcome or uninvited; and
- whether the conduct unreasonably interfered with the employee's work performance.

Harassment can be verbal, written, or physical

Verbal abuse may be the most common kind of harassment. This type of harassment consists of racial and ethnic epithets, slurs, demeaning impersonations or jokes directed at or made in the presence of persons with protected characteristics.

Verbal harassment can also be subtle. Comments that were never intended to show bias can still create a hostile work environment.

Verbal abuse does not have to result in psychological harm to cause a hostile work environment. Verbal abuse need only cause a work environment that would reasonably be perceived as, and is in fact perceived as, hostile or abusive.

Example: *Referring to male employees as "men" and female employees as "girls" may be gender harassment because the implication of female inferiority inherent in the different treatment can lead to a hostile or offensive work environment. Similarly, there may be racial or ethnic harassment when non-minority males are referred to as "men" while minority males are called "boy."*

Written abuse is just as inappropriate as verbal abuse. Demeaning or insulting drawings, cartoons, slogans, symbols and graffiti can also create an offensive environment and are inappropriate.

Email can be used as a tool to spread written abuse. Employees may be sending messages that contain material that is, or could be, interpreted as abusive, sexist, racist, or otherwise offensive.

This includes any messages with sexually suggestive material that is hostile to a particular gender or repeated and unwanted requests for a date.

The Internet allows users immediate access of information from around the world and has the potential for negative consequences in the workplace. Because the World Wide Web is not regulated, it contains information that some users may find offensive. Thus, there are areas on the Internet that are simply inappropriate for access by employees.

Employers should stress that equal opportunity and sexual harassment policies apply to email messages and Internet activities. Certain misuse can subject an employer to legal liability.

Protect yourself by never allowing Internet users to access sites with themes that are racist, sexist or otherwise discriminatory. Prohibit workers from downloading pornographic or violent material, such as sexually suggestive graphics or screen savers.

Physical or threatening behavior is also a form of harassment. Acts of intimidation have a threatening quality. The threats may be explicit or implicit. Threatening conduct is serious. When based on a protected characteristic, it may constitute unlawful harassment. Such behavior is highly inappropriate and should never be tolerated.

Inappropriate physical conduct may include obstructing a person's path, pushing, shoving, grabbing or touching. Destruction of a person's equipment or work product can also be harassment when done because a person belongs to a protected class.

Chapter 7—Harassment **157**

Remember Amy's supervisor, Frank? His misconduct fit all three kinds of harassment. Frank used verbal (vulgar language and repeatedly asking Amy to have sex) and written harassment (daily emails asking for a date) before escalating into physical conduct.

> ✓ **Checklist**
> **Examples of unlawful harassment:**
> ☐ Mimicking a worker's accent while criticizing his or her work performance.
> ☐ Copying the speech pattern of a person who has a cognitive disability while talking about the person in front of coworkers.
> ☐ Unwelcome sexually suggestive conduct or remarks.
> ☐ Circulating or displaying pictures or other items that are sexually suggestive or demeaning to a person because of his or her protected characteristic.
> ☐ Derogatory remarks about a person's age.
> ☐ Refusing to assist or cooperate in work that requires team effort because of another's protected characteristic.

Types of harassment

Harassment is not a "one size fits all" type of complaint. Harassers can belong to any protected category and can harass anyone in any protected category.

DON'T miss this

Sexual harassment

Sexual harassment is probably the type of harassment most people have heard about. Sexual harassment is unwelcome verbal or physical conduct of a sexual nature when:
1. submission to the conduct is made either an explicit or implicit term or condition of employment (such as promotion, training, timekeeping, overtime assignments, leaves of absence); *or*

2. submission to or rejection of the conduct is used as a basis for making employment decisions; *or*
3. the conduct has the purpose or effect of substantially interfering with an individual's work performance, or creating an intimidating, hostile, or offensive work environment.

Sexual harassment is not confined to men harassing women. Both men and women can be victims of sexual harassment and a harasser can be either a man or a woman. It is also unlawful for a man to sexually harass another man or for a woman to sexually harass another woman. The issue is whether the harasser is treating the victim in a particular way because of his or her gender.

Other types of harassment

Nonsexual harassment of an employee because of the employee's gender is also unlawful, as is harassment on the basis of any other protected category. Harassment on the basis of race, color, religion, national origin, gender, disability, or age exists when:
1. an employee is subjected to verbal or physical conduct that shows hostility toward the employee because of the employee's race, color, religion, national origin, gender, disability, or age; *and*
2. the conduct has the purpose or effect of interfering with the employee's work performance or opportunities, creating an intimidating, hostile or offensive work environment.

Example 1: *Allowing a supervisor to proselytize to an employee, leading that employee to believe that her job security could be affected by her reaction to the supervisor's discussion of his religious conviction, may amount to religious harassment.*

Example 2: *A 55-year-old female bank teller whose coworkers openly and frequently make jokes about her age and her medical problems, even after she has asked them to stop and has complained to her supervisor, may be the victim of age harassment.*

Chapter 7—Harassment

> **Example 3:** A woman with Downs Syndrome works as part of the clean-up crew at a fast-food restaurant. Her coworkers constantly torment her, hiding her supplies, calling her "Dumbo" and "retard." This conduct, if persistent and pervasive, could be unlawful disability harassment.
>
> **Example 4:** A lesbian is the target of anti-homosexual propaganda, hate mail, and crude jokes via e-mail. Although federal law does not protect workers from harassment on the basis of sexual orientation, a number of states and localities do have laws that prohibit sexual orientation harassment.

Remember, HR can set higher standards for employees that exceed the limits on workplace behavior allowed by law. Not all conduct that is vulgar or offensive is also illegal, but HR need not tolerate such behavior. Any time offensive conduct is allowed in the workplace, the employer risks disruption, lost productivity, poor morale, and the potential expense of litigation.

DON'T miss this

Harassers can be coworkers, supervisors or outsiders

Employers should also be aware that potential harassers could fit any job category or job level. A harasser can be a coworker, a supervisor or manager or an outsider who does business with the employer.

Coworker harassment

An employer will be liable for the actions of coworkers that create a hostile work environment in either of the following circumstances:
- ◆ The employer knew or should have known that harassment was taking place and failed to take immediate action to stop the harassment. Knowledge may come from a complaint made to management, firsthand observation, or a formal charge of harassment to the Equal Employment Opportunity Commission or local agency responsible for equal employment opportunity. Harassment that is openly

practiced in the workplace or is well-known among employees will be assumed to be known by the employer.
◆ The employer did not establish and distribute an explicit policy against harassment and did not provide a reasonable avenue for victims to complain to someone with authority to investigate and remedy the problem. The company will be held liable even if unaware of the conduct; in other words, whether it knew of the conduct or not.

Supervisor harassment

An employer can be held vicariously liable for the misconduct of a manager or supervisor.

> Vicarious liability means that an employer will be *automatically* liable for a manager's or supervisor's misconduct, even if no one in human resources or management knew about the harassment. The employer will be treated as if it engaged in the wrongdoing itself.

Because managers and supervisors have authority over employment decisions, their harassing conduct is more likely to intimidate employees and interfere with their work performance. Employees are less likely to complain or ask a manager to stop harassing conduct.

The severity of inappropriate conduct is increased when committed by a manager or supervisor because statements made by managers or supervisors can be directly attributed to the employer. Managers and supervisors are considered to be "agents" of the employer and any statement made by them can be used as evidence to show that an employer acted improperly. That's why it's so important that managers and supervisors be trained on their responsibilities to avoid and prevent harassment in the workplace (See "How can an employer protect itself?" below.)

Outsider or third party harassment

Employers must also understand that they could be held legally responsible for harassment committed by outsiders or "third parties" in the workplace. Harassment can come from outsiders such as customers, vendors, sales representatives, or even repair workers.

Chapter 7—Harassment

In determining whether an employer should be responsible for harassment by a third party, courts will look at whether:
- the employer knew or should have known of the conduct;
- the employer has some control over the situation or was otherwise legally responsible for the nonemployee's conduct; and
- the employer failed to take immediate and appropriate corrective action.

A bookstore cashier complained several times to her manager that a regular customer made sexual comments to her, kept asking her out on dates, and tried to grab her from behind four times. Because the store manager knew about the customer's behavior and did nothing about the cashier's complaints, the bookstore's owner could be held liable for the customer's conduct.

Rude conduct isn't necessarily harassment

Not all conduct that is offensive or even vulgar violates the law. However, tolerating offensive conduct because you don't think it's severe enough to constitute unlawful harassment is never a good idea.

Even if rude treatment of employees in the workplace does not meet the legal definitions of harassment, the conduct still should not be tolerated.

Any time offensive conduct is allowed in the workplace, an employer risks the disruption and expense of a harassment lawsuit. Depending on its severity, the conduct may even violate a criminal statute. Employers should also be aware that an employee who finds the conduct so intolerable that he or she quits might bring a constructive discharge lawsuit claiming that the workplace had become so oppressive that he or she was "forced out."

What if nobody has complained?

What if a supervisor has not received a complaint but suspects that harassment or other improper behavior is going on?

Regardless of how the supervisor became aware of the suspected misconduct, the supervisor must *immediately* and *confidentially* notify the person designated by company policy to investigate improper behavior. Even if the suspected misconduct seems welcome or involves persons who work in another department, the supervisor must still report it.

Reporting the suspected misconduct will ensure that a thorough investigation will take place and that appropriate corrective action will be taken if the investigation confirms the supervisor's suspicions. By taking such action, legal problems can be avoided.

On the other hand, failure of the supervisor to report the conduct can result in liability for an employer. For example, a company will be held liable for sexual harassment if a supervisor knew about the harassment but ignored it.

How can an employer protect itself?

Employers can reduce the chance of liability for harassment by taking all steps necessary to prevent harassment from occurring. Preventive measures would include:

- adopting an explicit policy against harassment;
- regularly communicating the policy to employees;
- training all supervisory and nonsupervisory employees and expressing strong disapproval for harassment;
- developing appropriate sanctions for harassment and communication of those sanctions to all employees; and
- implementing an effective grievance procedure for harassment complaints.

Take complaints about improper behavior seriously

Even if the person who complains about harassment or other rude conduct is a chronic complainer or if the behavior initially does not seem to be improper, take the complaint seriously.

Further investigation may reveal that the conduct is unlawful or against company policy.

If the employee quits because he or she has come away with the impression that the company did not take the complaint seriously, the employer could face a constructive discharge lawsuit.

Listen attentively and refrain from making any comments. Show the employee that the complaint is taken seriously by listening attentively and do not make comments like "you're overreacting—I'm sure no harm was intended."

Implement anti-harassment policy and grievance procedure

One very important step an employer can take is implementing an anti-harassment policy and grievance procedure. The anti-harassment policy and grievance procedure must include an assurance that a harassing supervisor can be bypassed to register a complaint. If employees are completely isolated from higher management, an employer exposes itself to liability despite a chain of command grievance procedure.

Anti-harassment policy. A policy that prohibits harassment in the workplace is an integral part of any organization's efforts to create a bias-free workplace.

The creation and distribution of an adequate policy is one of the most crucial steps that can be taken to prevent workplace harassment and to avoid liability should unlawful behavior occur.

A company that does not establish and distribute a clear policy against workplace harassment—and provide a reasonable avenue for victims to complain to someone with authority to investigate and remedy the problem—may be held liable for unlawful harassment regardless of whether it knew of the conduct.

In order to ensure a work environment that is free from harassment and any other form of discrimination, put in place a policy that encourages *respect* in the workplace. And make sure that the policy is written so that all employees can understand it.

WHAT you need to know

Harassment prevention policy

There are several provisions that you should include in your policy against discrimination and harassment. The most important provisions are:

- a clear prohibition against harassment and discrimination;
- an effective procedure for reporting harassment or other inappropriate behavior;
- a clear prohibition against retaliation;
- a description of the investigation process;
- confidentiality expectations for all persons involved in process; and
- an explanation of discipline that could be issued if misconduct is found.

DON'T miss this

Employer should be aware that there are states which have specific laws or regulations about posting sexual harassment guidelines. There are also states which require employers to implement a sexual harassment policy. Be sure to check your state law for any requirements you may have to fulfill.

Communicate the anti-harassment policy to employees

An anti-harassment policy is worth nothing if no one knows anything about it. An employer must ensure that all its employees, supervisors and managers are aware of the anti-harassment policy through verbal and written means.

WHAT you need to know

Employees, supervisors, and managers should be trained as part of their orientation to the company. That training should be periodically updated (for example, conduct an annual anti-harassment workshop).

If a harassment complaint is made or is observed, it may be necessary to re-train the entire workforce or those who may be lacking in the necessary understanding of appropriate behavior.

If a complaint is found to have merit, this is a clear warning signal that training efforts should be reevaluated for effectiveness.

Remember Amy? She did not know what to do about being sexually harassed by her supervisor. She did not know if her employer had an anti-harassment policy and she did not know who to tell about her supervisor's harassment. Her lack of knowledge could be a big problem for her employer (1) if no anti-harassment policy exists or (2) if an anti-harassment policy exists but she never heard about it.

There many methods that can be used to communicate an anti-harassment policy including an employee handbook, a handout included with a paycheck, a written notice posted on bulletin board, a workshop or training seminar on harassment.

Grievance procedure. Employees must know how to bring their concerns and complaints about harassment to someone's attention. Select several job positions for employees to take their complaints. It is logical to choose a department's supervisor or manager as the person to receive complaints. However, if that supervisor or manager is the harasser, employees will need another person to take their complaint to.

If no effective complaint procedure is in place, it is reasonable for employees to believe that harassment will be ignored, tolerated or even condoned by management.

Additionally, when a supervisor engages in sexual or other unlawful harassment, the employer likely will be automatically liable if no policy against harassment has been established and if there is no system to allow victims to complain to someone with the authority to investigate and remedy the problem.

And even if the harasser is a coworker or nonemployee, the employer may still be liable because it "should have known" of the harassment, but did not know only because the employee had no effective means to report it.

On the other hand, an effective complaint procedure that encourages employees to complain about sexual or other unlawful harassment puts the employer in a stronger position to defend against a harassment claim. In the case of harassment by a manager or supervisor, the employer may be able to escape otherwise automatic liability. And, if a complaining employee has no legitimate reason for failing to use the complaint procedure, his or her credibility may be damaged.

It is also more difficult to claim that harassment forced an employee to quit the job if the employee did not use an effective complaint procedure before quitting.

Investigate complaints

A thorough investigation of an employee's harassment complaint can make all the difference. Any employer who fails to adequately investigate a complaint is setting itself up for a lawsuit and, possibly, loss of that lawsuit.

Best Practices

Ensuring a thorough investigation

The steps to ensuring a thorough investigation of a harassment complaint are simple and easy to understand.

- After a complaint has been made, thank the employee for bringing the complaint and assure him or her that no negative action will be taken against him or her for making the complaint.
- Ask for, but don't require, a written statement.
- Assure the employee his or her complaint will be handled as discreetly and confidentially as possible.
- Gather facts and find out:
  - who, what, when, where, why, and how;
  - are there any witnesses;

- is any documentation, such as letters, notes, or email messages that may support the complaint;
- is the employee afraid of retaliation from the person(s) who committed the alleged improper conduct.
♦ Ask what the employee what would he or she like to have happen to resolve the problem, but do not promise that is the action that will be taken. You should tell the employee there will be a prompt and thorough investigation and that appropriate remedial action will be taken if misconduct is found.
♦ Caution the employee he or she may be held personally liable for defamation if malicious or false statements are made during the investigation or if the matter is discussed with others.
♦ Be sure to carefully document all the information gathered from the employee and during your investigation.

An effective investigator must develop and maintain a current, in-depth understanding of all applicable sexual harassment laws, Equal Employment Opportunity Commission statements about sexual harassment, and significant developments in case law.

✓ Checklist

Choosing an effective investigator

An investigator should be able to:
- ☐ be objective and unbiased;
- ☐ treat sensitive information professionally and confidentially;
- ☐ comfortably discuss sensitive and highly personal matters, including explicit sexual behavior;
- ☐ be nonjudgmental and able to resist emotional involvement;
- ☐ distinguish facts from opinions;
- ☐ ask hard questions and to draw out honest answers;
- ☐ be thorough and attentive to detail; and
- ☐ understand the unique viewpoint of each interviewee and present differences of opinion from others for further comment.

Be discreet

The privacy rights of both the accuser and the accused must be respected at all times. Never discuss a complaint against an employee or information concerning the complaint with anyone who does not have a legitimate interest in and duty to receive the information. Ensure that all communications about the matter are strictly private and cannot be overheard. And never broadcast the results of an investigation as an example to others or as a training tool.

The Quiz

1. A man can be sexually harassed by a woman.   ❏ True   ❏ False

2. A hostile environment is where:
   a. an employee has been subjected to verbal or physical conduct that shows hostility toward an employee because of a protected characteristic.
   b. the conduct has the purpose or effect of interfering with the employee's work performance or opportunities, or creating an intimidating, hostile or offensive work environment.
   c. both A and B.
   d. none of the above.

3. An employer can be held automatically liable when a supervisor harasses an employee.   ❏ True   ❏ False

4. All offensive and rude behavior is harassment.   ❏ True   ❏ False

5. An anti-harassment policy and a grievance procedure can help protect an employer from harassment claims.   ❏ True   ❏ False

Answer Key: 1. T; 2. C; 3. T; 4. F; 5. T

Chapter 8

Discipline

Who's responsible for discipline?...	170
What makes a good disciplinary system?...............................	170
Communication is the key...	174
Supervisor as coach...	175
What good is an investigation?...	177
Documenting the discipline process...	183
What documentation can do for you..	185
BEST PRACTICES: Involve the employee............................	191
The Quiz...	193

> *The work performance of two of your best employees has suddenly taken a noticeable turn for the worse. Doris and Angie were top performers under the old system but are now two of the worst performers. Their manager has just told you that he's going to fire them at the end of the day because "they know better." What do you do?*

Who's responsible for discipline?

Since supervisors and managers are the company representatives in direct contact with employees, they are the individuals with immediate responsibility for discipline. However, disciplining employees is usually one part of the job that supervisors don't enjoy. Some hate confrontation and would rather avoid dealing directly with employees. Others worry about problems developing if they make a mistake during the process.

HR can ease the pain by providing a support system for supervisors.

How far the immediate supervisor can go in the discipline process without bringing in HR or a higher-level manager is determined by each organization. However, routine discussions of disciplinary action with HR and upper management are beneficial, not only a courtesy, but also because they help track an employee's disciplinary record if he or she transfers to another department. In addition, such discussions provide guidance, support, and often a necessary perspective to the immediate supervisor.

What makes a good disciplinary system?

A good disciplinary system is one that is fair and consistent. The same type of misconduct should be treated in the same manner, no matter how favored—or disfavored—the employee may be. The same can be said for performance issues.

Sometimes after an employee has been disciplined, he or she may feel "singled out" or slighted. The employee may even consult an attorney to discuss the situation.

Having a good disciplinary system in place can help reduce the chances that your organization may be sued.

Components of effective disciplinary system

A good disciplinary system has several components:
1. a code of conduct,
2. a philosophy of discipline,
3. knowledge of the consequences of misconduct,
4. consistent discipline procedures,
5. quick response,
6. review of planned discipline, and
7. an appeal procedure.

1. A code of conduct. A disciplinary system should be fair and consistent. A good and fair disciplinary system should let employees know what behavior is expected and what behavior is unacceptable.

> Employees should receive this information, preferably in writing, at their orientation and leave with a copy to keep.

Work rules are the foundation of a disciplinary system. If an employee does not know what is expected, how can the employee live up to the employer's expectations? Moreover, work rules should include a clear idea of what will happen if they are not followed. Never divorce the work rules from the consequences for an infraction.

It is a good idea to have a system in place to prove that employees were told what the rules are. Many organizations accomplish this by asking their employees to sign a statement acknowledging receipt of the work rules. Or HR can note an employee's receipt of work rules in the employee's personnel file.

> *Work rules can be included in an employee handbook, posted on a bulletin board or intranet, or distributed to employees in any other way that is effective. To ensure that employees know the rules, they should be redistributed periodically. Some organizations republish their work rules annually whether the rules have been revised or not.*

2. A philosophy of discipline. Your company's philosophy of discipline sets the tone for everything that follows. Everyone involved must understand the company's goals when implementing discipline or the company risks sending the wrong message. There are two systems of discipline that an employer can use, punitive and corrective.

> In a **punitive** discipline system, the purpose of punishment is to reinforce the work rules or desired conduct by making the consequences for nonperformance unpleasant.
>
> In a **corrective** discipline system, a supervisor coaches the employee toward improved performance and may try to find out why the employee's behavior is off track. The supervisor explains the desired behavior, gives suggestions for ways to improve and sets a timeline for monitoring improvement. Progressive discipline is a system of behavior improvement that uses progressive steps in the process.

3. Knowledge of the consequences of misconduct. Supervisors and employees alike should clearly understand the consequences of misconduct or other inappropriate conduct. Consequences of misconduct should be interwoven with other employment policies, such as attendance, sexual harassment and violence in the workplace.

> *Do not cut off the consequences of rule violations from the policies themselves. Employees should know what penalty the employer will impose for common offenses.*

4. Consistent discipline procedures. It cannot be stressed enough that discipline, whatever your approach, must be consistent to be fair. Lack of a fair and consistent application of discipline is the reason underlying many, if not most, lawsuits brought by employees against their employers.

Chapter 8—Discipline

When contemplating disciplinary action, keep in mind the golden rule of discipline: What would you do if this were your best employee?

The discipline process must be monitored to ensure consistency and compliance across the organization.

5. Quick response. Imposing discipline is never convenient or pleasant. Everyone has a lot of work to do and meetings to attend, so the temptation may be great to ignore problems until they become the "straw that breaks the camel's back."

But ignoring or postponing necessary disciplinary action just makes things worse. To be effective, discipline must follow as closely to the misconduct as possible. Employees should expect a quick response by their supervisor or leader to violations of the code of conduct.

6. Review of planned discipline. Whenever discipline involves significant consequences to the employee, a second or third opinion is a good idea. By reviewing the facts of an incident and a supervisor's proposed course action, HR can help the supervisor prepare to act on the decision, both procedurally and emotionally.

7. Appeal procedure. An appeal procedure injects added integrity into disciplinary proceedings, making the overall discipline process fairer and less arbitrary.

Employees should have an opportunity to appeal any disciplinary action through an established appeal process that includes management and the HR staff. In some organizations, discipline decisions can be appealed to a review board that also includes the appealing party's peers.

Communication is the key

The process of ongoing review and dialogue should be part of the supervisor/employee relationship. Often, employees become poor performers simply because there is no communication from their supervisors. They think that their conduct or performance is satisfactory, when it is not. Only when "the last straw" is reached will a supervisor initiate a performance discussion. By then, it may be too late and the organization may lose a valuable employee.

How can HR help?

HR can come to the aid of the organization by not only explaining the importance of continuing communication about performance to supervisors, but by coaching supervisors on how to talk about performance constructively. Supervisors must advise employees when they are not meeting the performance and conduct requirements of their positions so they can take the corrective action needed to improve.

Periodic, scheduled meetings are needed to check the employee's progress, set new goals if needed and to give encouragement where improvement is seen. HR can be instrumental in this process by assisting in scheduling the meetings, providing role-playing opportunities to rehearse the performance discussions, and following up to see that communication continues.

One of the most important elements in an effective progressive discipline system is clear and direct communication. Supervisors must explain to the employee:
- the perceived problem,
- possible solutions, and
- management's expectations.

Is training the problem?

When an employee performs poorly, it may not always be a discipline problem. HR should remind any supervisor confronting a performance problem to take a good look at whether the poor performance is caused by improper or inadequate training that leaves the employee unable to perform the job.

*One expert advises supervisors to ask whether the employee **could** do the job if his or her life depended upon it.*

Training is the solution to a performance problem if the employee lacks the basic skills or knowledge to do a job. If the person had done the job satisfactorily in the past but is not doing it now, however, there is no training problem. In such cases it is appropriate to try to improve performance with counseling and progressive discipline.

Remember Doris and Angie? They were top performers before the company switched to a new system. It's important for HR to check into the training the women received on the new system.

The first question to ask is "were they trained?" HR would then want to check into the specifics of the training and if it were comparable to the training other employees received. Doris and Angie's recent poor performance could simply be a matter of inadequate training. If so, your problem is easily solved and you don't lose two of your best employees.

Supervisor as coach

A progressive discipline system is meant to bring about improvement, not to punish. In such a system, the supervisor's role is to coach the employee to peak performance. The employee's role is to take responsibility for improving his or her performance to meet the stated expectations of the organization.

HR's role is to provide support and guidance for both of them, ensuring that organization policy and legal requirements are followed in the process.

The supervisor should work with the employee to correct unacceptable behavior. To do so, HR and the supervisor will want to explore the reasons behind the unacceptable behavior. By knowing the cause of the problem, the employee and supervisor can then be guided to work together toward a solution.

There can be many causes behind unacceptable behavior or performance, and in many cases the solution may be simple:
- If an employee is habitually tardy because of childcare responsibilities, perhaps a change in scheduling is the solution.
- An employee whose focus and productivity have slipped after the recent death of a loved one may benefit from an Employee Assistance Program.
- An employee with diabetes who is experiencing fatigue may need more frequent meal breaks.

HR's knowledge and insights into the organization's past practice, available options, and compliance concerns makes HR's involvement critical in exploring the reasons behind unacceptable behavior.

Power of positive reinforcement. As supervisors move through a progressive discipline system, they must remember to encourage the employee whenever improvement is shown, even if the improvement is small and there is still room for greater improvement. A good coach rewards employees' efforts at behavioral improvement with sincere praise and smiles. Even when things are not going so well in the progressive discipline process, effective supervisors find something positive to say and reassure the employee that the supervisor is rooting for him or her to succeed.

Maybe the employee won't make it, but the employee needs to see that his or her supervisor believes he or she can!

Consistency counts. While supervisors may be tempted to play favorites or to give their star employees "a pass," supervisors must take the same approach to discipline with all employees. If one employee gets a friendly reminder about being late while another employee gets a written warning, there is inconsistent treatment. The employee who gets the written warning may think this inconsistent treatment is based on an unlawful motive such as race or sex discrimination.

What good is an investigation?

An important part of any disciplinary system is the investigation process. Investigations can help HR discover the reasons for an employee's poor performance. In the case of Doris and Angie, an investigation led HR to discover inadequate training was the cause of their poor performance. An investigation could have also led HR to discover other reasons for the women's poor performance such as misconduct or safety concerns.

The point is, you'll never know the reasons for your employees actions if you don't use some type of investigative to find out.

Investigation basics

When in response to a complaint, investigation can help determine if misconduct occurred and, if it did, who is responsible. An investigation will also help lessen the chance that disciplinary action will be taken against the wrong individual or used arbitrarily.

There are several basic factors to consider before starting an investigation:

- assess the situation;
- decide whether a formal or informal investigation is best; and
- decide who should conduct the investigation.

Assess the situation. The kind of "investigation" that is required before a decision to impose discipline is made will vary with each situation. Sometimes the "investigation" is not really an investigation at all, but an informal discussion that clarifies a misunderstanding.

Sometimes, the actual facts are not in question and very little is required in terms of investigating what took place. Even if this is the case, an "investigation" or review should be undertaken before any disciplinary action is taken.

Determine proper organizational policy and procedure and how it was used in the past to ensure that discipline is fairly and consistently applied. Ask yourself: Is the problem a discipline situation? Have others engaged in similar misconduct? If so, how was it handled? Is there anything that makes this situation unique?

The best place to start any investigation is with the basic facts. Carefully analyze the facts of each situation. HR can help direct the focus of the analysis and determine whether the situation is disciplinary or whether you're dealing with something else, such as a medical condition that may require accommodation or a problem that could be solved with better training.

Each rule infraction or allegation of misconduct needs to be carefully evaluated. HR can and should help supervisors recommend behavior changes or warn employees when appropriate, but it is equally important that HR makes sure that the reason for the misconduct is not related to a protected trait or right.

Decide whether a formal or informal investigation is best. A formal internal investigation can be time-consuming, costly and take up valuable resources. Therefore, it is HR's job to know the kinds of situations that demand formal investigation and those that can be resolved in a more informal manner. After all, it is to everyone's benefit to reach a solution that is acceptable to all in the most efficient and effective manner.

The kinds of problems that frequently can be resolved informally involve misunderstandings over the organization's policies, standards and work rules. In these cases it is the expectations of the organization, often the employee's immediate supervisor, and the employee that are at issue. HR can quickly clarify any misinformation that the employee has received.

A more formal investigation is needed when you don't have all of the facts. A formal investigation is advisable if the situation involves more than one employee, if there is a pattern of unacceptable conduct, if the nature of the conduct is severe, or if you need help from someone with special expertise (for example, corporate counsel, security, risk management, auditors) to reach a conclusion. A formal investigation would also be necessary if you need to examine and review documents and other evidence.

Who should conduct the investigation?

> *An employee's immediate supervisor should not conduct the investigation.*

The right person to conduct an investigation is someone who is impartial but knowledgeable of the organization's policies, procedures, and operations. In many cases that person will come from HR. It is important, however, that HR professionals be thoroughly trained before undertaking investigative duties. In larger firms, HR may coordinate investigations with in-house counsel and/or the security department, especially if those departments contain staff with prior law enforcement background and training.

Another alternative is to ask an outside attorney to conduct the investigation. Although an expensive option, putting an attorney in charge may show that the organization wants objectivity and is concerned about the seriousness of the offense. This is particularly true when investigating sexual harassment or corporate corruption because the organization's own employees can appear to be interested only in vindicating the organization. If a member of senior management is the target of the investigation, utilizing outside attorneys may be the best strategy to avoid conflict of interest charges.

> Be aware that use of an outside organization to conduct an investigation of a disciplinary claim may trigger obligations under the Fair Credit Reporting Act.

Counseling interviews

Counseling interviews utilize interviewing skills that require a great deal of practice, and some supervisors may never master the required skills. Some may also have personal qualities that make it difficult for them to be effective in such a role. HR can help supervisors develop and refine their skills with training and role-playing exercises. In addition, it may be helpful for HR to take the counseling role.

It is necessary to be aware of the employee's background and to have assessed his or her temperament beforehand, adjusting the interview situation to suit.

However, as counseling is a "discovery" exercise in which personal disclosures can be made, planning can only be done to a limited extent.

Counseling interviews combine investigation with an attempt to change the underlying behavior. Such interviews are most successful if the focus is on joint problem-solving rather than judging or blaming, if specific factual observations are made rather than generalizations or conclusions, and if employees are given the opportunity to explain their perspectives.

Accident investigations

Accident investigations should be conducted by individuals with specialized knowledge. In large organizations this responsibility is usually assigned to a safety director. In smaller firms, the supervisor of the affected area or employee may be responsible for the investigation. HR is often part of an accident investigation team.

The primary focus of an accident investigation should be on why the accident or near miss occurred and what actions can be taken to prevent a recurrence.

While recommended preventative measures often involve disciplinary actions, discipline is not always the solution. Sometimes the investigation will lead to recommendations for a change in operational procedures or policy.

Harassment investigations

Harassment investigations pose special challenges, but there can be special rewards for the employer. Although an employer is automatically liable if a supervisor's harassing conduct involves a tangible employment action like a discharge or a demotion, a prompt and appropriate response when employers know of harassing conduct by coworkers will help employers defend against claims of hostile environment harassment.

The first response to a report of harassment should be a prompt and thorough investigation. The results of the investigation will dictate the appropriate response, which may or may not involve disciplinary action.

Employee representation at investigations

Whether or not an employee can take a representative into a discipline meeting depends in large part on whether or not the workplace is unionized. If the workplace is unionized, chances are that employer and employee rights are spelled out in a collective bargaining agreement. Even if the agreement doesn't specifically spell out an employee's right to representation at a discipline meeting, unionized employees have a limited right to have such representation. And in 2000 that limited right to representation was extended to nonunion employees.

Employees may seek to have a representative present only at "investigatory interviews"—no right to representation exists at purely disciplinary meetings that are solely for the purpose of informing the employee of a previously made disciplinary decision and action upon that decision.

Disability-related inquiries

The Americans with Disabilities Act restricts the type of questions that an employer may ask current employees. Employees cannot be asked if they have a disability or about the nature or severity of a disability unless the inquiry is job-related and consistent with business necessity. It stands to reason that an inquiry that is not job-related serves no legitimate employer purpose. However, it does serve to stigmatize the person with a disability.

DON'T miss this

A "disability-related" inquiry is one that is likely to elicit information about a disability. When HR or a supervisor is conducting an investigation in the context of imposing discipline, care must be exercised to not ask questions that will obtain information about a disability.

✓ Checklist
Impermissible disability-related questions

- ☐ Asking an employee whether he or she has (or ever had) a disability.
- ☐ Asking an employee about the nature or severity of the employee's disability.
- ☐ Asking an employee to provide medical documentation regarding his or her disability.
- ☐ Asking an employee whether he or she currently is taking any prescription drugs or medications, or monitoring an employee's taking of such drugs or medications.
- ☐ Asking an employee a broad question about his or her impairments that is likely to elicit information about a disability.

The following questions are permitted:
- ☐ Asking generally about an employee's well being.
- ☐ Asking an employee whether he or she can perform job functions.
- ☐ Asking an employee whether he or she has been drinking.
- ☐ Asking an employee about his or her current illegal use of drugs.

Job-related and consistent with business necessity. A disability-related inquiry may be "job-related and consistent with business necessity" when an employer has a reasonable belief, based on objective evidence, that:

1. an employee's ability to perform essential job functions will be impaired by a medical condition; or
2. an employee will pose a direct threat (to self or others) due to a medical condition.

Known disabilities. Sometimes the standard (of job-related and consistent with business necessity) may be met when an employer knows about a particular employee's medical condition, has observed performance problems, and reasonably can attribute the problems to the medical condition.

Third-party information. Disability-related inquiries may also be asked on the basis of reliable information obtained from a third party. Factors that might affect whether or not information that is learned from another person is sufficient to justify asking disability-related questions include:
- the relationship between the person providing the information to the employee about whom it is being provided;
- the seriousness of the medical condition at issue;
- the possible motivation of the person providing the information;
- how the person learned the information (from the person whose medical condition is in question or from someone else?); and
- other evidence that bears on the reliability of the information provided.

Documenting the discipline process

Documentation is an essential element of any human resources program, but it is especially critical in the discipline process. It helps managers and supervisors support personnel decisions and substantiate any disciplinary actions. Documentation also plays an important role in performance appraisals, feedback between managers and employees, and in training. There are many good reasons for managers and supervisors to document actions taken while managing people.

Evidence. Personnel decisions are less subject to challenge and, when challenged, are more easily defended with documentation. In court cases and unemployment hearings, if an organization's documentation is not timely, accurate and written to address the problem, the organization is likely to lose.

Performance improvement. Documentation can provide a written set of goals or objectives that an employee must meet to improve performance.

A written set of performance goals or standards can prevent misunderstandings about what an employee must accomplish to improve performance and avoid disciplinary action.

Communication. The process of ongoing review and dialogue should be part of the manager/employee relationship. The use of documentation can improve feedback between a manager and an employee.

Record of personnel actions. When managers need to substantiate their actions to others they use documentation. If disciplinary action is questioned, documentation will be the key to supporting that action.

Notice to the employee. Documentation provides evidence that an employee was actually or constructively aware of the rules, verification that the employee heard and understood the rules and policies, and is evidence that an organization's policies have been applied and enforced consistently. Documentation will help to support a manager's position that the manager did or did not do something.

Generally, employees are not bound by rules that have not been brought to their attention, nor should they be punished for conduct that they did not reasonably understand was a problem.

Guidelines for future performance. Documentation eliminates any possible misunderstanding concerning work rules. A manager can clearly state what is expected of an employee in the future and to describe to the employee the consequences of future infractions. For example, when a manager becomes aware of unsatisfactory performance, documentation can provide evidence that an employee was accorded progressive discipline, was adequately warned about poor performance and had a reasonable opportunity to improve.

Training and development. Documentation can also be used as a record of an employee's training and development, how an employee performed during training and the employee's career goals.

What documentation can do for you

Documentation is especially important when discipline is involved. When disciplinary decisions are being made, documentation is critical because it can show that:

- **Employer policies were followed.** Documentation can indicate that an employee knew the policy existed and can show whether the manager warned the employee about violating the policy. Also, it can indicate whether there were any mitigating circumstances and whether disciplinary policies and procedures were followed.
- There was a **valid business purpose** for the discipline, and that the action does not violate any law, policy or employment agreement.
- A **thorough investigation** was conducted and employees were given the opportunity to relate their side of the story.
- Support exists in the employee's overall **personnel record** for the discipline decision. It substantiates the fact that an employee was told how to improve, when improvement was needed, and the consequences of a failure to improve.
- If **accommodation** is an issue, documentation can provide evidence that an employer made an offer of reasonable accommodation, taking into account a person's religion or disability.
- **Treatment was evenhanded.** Documentation can provide evidence that employees who have engaged in similar conduct were subject to similar discipline, thus supporting the position that an employee's protected status (for example, race, religion, sex, national origin, etc.) had nothing to do with the decision to discipline.

This is really the bottom line—documents are evidence that can absolve you and the organization from liability.

How to document

An organization's managers and supervisors need the ability to create a well-written, clear and convincing document that will withstand review and challenge. But, as HR professionals know, knowing how to create good documentation isn't an inborn trait that comes with the promotion to management. One way for HR to prove its value to an organization is to assist management in developing effective documentation.

> **✓ Checklist**
>
> **Important questions documentation should answer**
>
> Every organization has its own documentation format and procedures, but there are common elements that are found in all good documentation. Stress to managers and supervisors you need their documentation to answer the five Ws: who, what, where, when and why.
>
> - ☐ **Who** was involved in the incident? Who witnessed it? Who is administering discipline?
> - ☐ **What** behavior is causing the problem? What can be done to correct it? What behavior is expected in the future? What are the consequences for engaging in the undesired behavior?
> - ☐ **Where** did the incident take place?
> - ☐ **When** did the incident take place?
> - ☐ **Why** is the behavior inappropriate? Why is discipline warranted?

Does it matter which format is used?

There are several documentation methods that can be used, from supervisors writing a short summary to reporting on each behavioral incident. Summaries can be supported with some specific examples. Single-incident documentation can be used where an employee may have limited opportunity to perform a particular task during the year.

Customized forms. Though the simplest method, using a memo or "blank sheet" format to document discipline is very difficult.

A better approach is for an organization to establish its own format and make preprinted documentation forms available to its managers and supervisors.

Generally, organizations provide a form that incorporates a significant amount of space to customize the form to the individual situation. Nonetheless, the elements in the checklist above should be included, even merely as "titles" to sections of blank space, to prompt the person creating the documentation to "cover all the bases."

Checkbox for infractions. It is common for forms to have checkbox listings of frequent types of infractions, such as:
- Substandard work
- Conduct
- Carelessness
- Disobedience
- Tardiness
- Violation of work rule (specify the work rule)
- Other (please explain).

These forms frequently include blank space to write in the specifics or amplify the importance of the violation.

Paper or digital. Documentation can be completed by hand or on the computer and may be retained in hard copy, a database, or both. Forms can be printed on multiple-part paper, providing a copy for the employee, the supervisor and the personnel file.

Verbal warnings need documentation too. Not documenting verbal warnings is a dangerous practice. If an employee asserts that discipline was arbitrary and unfair, proper documentation can show that it was appropriate and carried out according to your organization's established rules for discipline. But doesn't that make this a written warning?

No. A verbal warning does not require documentation of the entire conversation like a written warning would, but to document a verbal warning keep a record, perhaps on your calendar, of when you spoke to the employee and when you agreed to meet again.

HR How-to: EMPLOYMENT LAW

Worst case scenario
Supervisor doesn't want to document

Tristan is a good employee. He's reasonably productive, well liked, and respected by coworkers. Carmen has stated that he's been stopping by her office every day, asking her to join him for coffee or lunch. When she says no, he smiles and says "maybe tomorrow." She has complained to Tristan's supervisor, Robert, that Tristan "bothers" her.

Robert and Tristan have a good relationship and Robert was able to take Tristan aside and ask him to "leave Carmen alone." Robert thinks this is the end of the matter–that he doesn't have to document employee actions unless the employee might be terminated. Since everything seems OK now, Robert is ready to move on without doing anything further.

Solution: Explain to Robert that documentation of performance and disciplinary problems has greater value than just the creation of a paper trail in support of termination decisions. Robert should be trained on how to use documentation to improve communication with employees and to establish employee goals.

Robert could also benefit from a refresher course on the organization's sexual harassment policy. Documentation showing an employer's prompt response to a complaint of sexual harassment can help to limit the organization's liability should Carmen decide to file sexual harassment charges.

Be sure documentation is timely. To ensure accuracy, documentation should be created as soon as possible. It can be as simple as jotting down quick notes of the time and place of the event, whether the observed behavior was appropriate and whether the action taken was effective. This helps to remember the event. These notes then can be used to write either a short, hand-written summary or a more extensive report on the situation, including witness statements and supporting evidence.

Date every document used in the process. It sounds like something that should not have to be said; however, it is not uncommon to find personnel files loaded with documentation that has not been dated. For some kinds of documentation, the absence of a date renders a document useless.

Dating all documentation is important; if warnings are not dated, their usefulness is greatly diminished. For example, when defending a disciplinary action, it is useful to show when the employee was given written warnings. If the warnings were given a short time before the disciplinary action, they are persuasive. If, on the other hand, the warnings were given two years earlier, and the employee had no further violations until the time of the disciplinary action, the warnings may no longer be relevant.

> *Dates are also important to help refresh the memory of the individual who wrote them. By arranging the documentation chronologically, a pattern can be quickly and easily discovered.*

Relevance of prior violations. Prior violations, if any, should be addressed, but only those that have been documented and are relevant to the infraction currently being documented. If a prior violation was not documented at the time, then it should not be used in a subsequent situation. Likewise, if the prior documentation has no meaning or impact to the current situation, it is not appropriate to automatically include the information. Each situation requires objective review and judgment.

Documentation should be detail-oriented and objective. Good documentation shows what led up to the disciplinary action taken. It should include notes about who HR or the investigator spoke to, what was learned, and what physical evidence was found.

> Stress to your supervisors and managers that HR needs documentation that is specific and objective.

Be specific. Many supervisors and managers, because of time constraints, lack of writing ability, or not knowing any better, tend to make broad general statements when documenting an employee's performance. Good documentation is specific and objective. It should not contain broad, general statements or unsupported conclusions. Instead, it needs to deal with the facts and tell a story.

Supervisors and managers tend to "beat around the bush." The better approach is to be direct and to write clearly and concisely. Rather than saying that the employee's work is sloppy, good documentation will specify what is wrong with the employee's work, for example, that it is incomplete, late—by how long—and contains specified errors.

Make sure that any description of employee misconduct focuses on the misconduct and is specific about the nature of the misconduct. Leave no room for doubt that discipline is being used because what the employee did violated established work rules and not because of who the employee is.

Be objective. The use of conclusory labels compromises the document's objectivity. Let's look at the case of Susie, whose supervisor comes to you with documentation that says Susie lied to him on Monday about why she didn't come to work on Friday. Is that good documentation? Can you even tell what happened from the supervisor's "documentation"? After talking with the supervisor you find out that last Friday Susie said that she couldn't come to work because her car wouldn't start. On Monday, her supervisor asked for a receipt showing that she had her car repaired, but she didn't have one.

A better way to document what happened would be to write:

> *"On Monday, March 6, 2003, Susie said she couldn't come to work last Friday because her car broke down. I asked her for receipts for repairs. She couldn't provide them. I asked her the name of the garage where the repairs were done and she said she couldn't remember."*

Best Practices

Involve the employee

Where possible, involve the employee in the actual documentation process, encouraging the employee to write summaries of manager-supervisor conferences and including these summaries as part of the official record. Employee input makes the process fairer. It may also increase an employee's "buy-in" and provide a greater likelihood that the employee will be successful in improving performance or otherwise changing behavior.

Alternatively, some forms include statements expressing the employee's agreement with the facts as stated in the documentation. These statements may be expressed as *"The absence of any employee statement indicates agreement with the facts as presented."* Sometimes employee agreement or disagreement is recorded by having the employee check a box that he or she agrees or disagrees with the facts as stated.

Throughout the disciplinary process, management should listen to the employee's side of the story. Doing so early on may eliminate the need for an appeal later. Don't miss the opportunity to "hear the employee out" and document what the employee says. Each disciplinary record should have a section referring to the employee that begins, "You said that ... "

Some disciplinary forms require employee signatures and provide the employee with a copy in order to show that the employee is on notice of what is wrong and what must be changed. It is common for a variation of the following language to appear above the employee signature: *My signature below acknowledges that I have been advised of the actions to be taken as a result of this reprimand. I have read this warning and understand it.*

Final review

Before documentation is placed in an employee's personnel file, it is a good idea to have another manager or an HR representative read and sign off on it. This final review ensures that documentation is complete and no improper comments are contained in the file.

It also ensures consistency with organizational policy and procedure, and that there is an accurate record that can be relied upon to explain the disciplinary action. The reviewer should be someone who is trained and familiar with both the laws under which an individual could bring a legal action as a result of disciplinary documentation and with your organization's policy.

Document communications with all employees! As is true with all aspects of discipline, consistency is critical with respect to documentation. When a situation is not documented consistently, the organization may not be able to defend itself if faced with a grievance, complaint or litigation. The lack of documentation might be used, for example, to show discriminatory intent, to show that the organization doesn't have employee relations programs, or to show that the organization acted in an arbitrary fashion.

The Quiz

1. Which of the following are parts of a good disciplinary system?
   a. A code of conduct.
   b. Knowledge of the consequences of misconduct.
   c. Consistent discipline procedures.
   d. All of the above.
   e. None of the above.

2. In a punitive disciplinary system, a supervisor explains the desired behavior and offers ways to improve. ☐ True ☐ False

3. The best place to start an investigation is a careful analysis of the facts. ☐ True ☐ False

4. Documentation is important because it can help support the reason for taking disciplinary action against an employee. ☐ True ☐ False

5. Good documentation:
   a. Is undated.
   b. Refers to every incident of prior misconduct committed by employee.
   c. Has specific and objective statements.
   d. All of the above.
   e. None of the above.

6. Verbal warnings do not have to be documented. ☐ True ☐ False

Answer key: 1. D; 2. F; 3. T; 4. T; 5. C; 6. F

Chapter 9

Employee relations

Employees' basic labor rights 196
What is protected activity? 199
Employer interference 200
Union activities 201
    BEST PRACTICES: Train supervisors
        to avoid committing unfair labor practices 203
    BEST PRACTICES: Preventive strategies
        to deter employees from contacting a union 208
The employee handbook 210
The Quiz 213

> *Kent worked on the day shift in the company warehouse for three years before being reassigned to the night shift. As part of a collective bargaining agreement, employees working the night shift are paid a higher rate. When his first paycheck did not reflect the change in pay, Kent approached his supervisor, Harry, to find out why. After some discussion, Harry told Kent he was not eligible for the higher pay rate. The conversation continued and became increasingly hostile before Kent started yelling expletives at Harry. Kent has stormed into your office saying Harry threatened to demote him for complaining about not getting the paid the higher night rate. Kent tells you Harry has violated his rights. Is he right?*

Employees' basic labor rights

Labor relations and collective bargaining are regulated by federal law, specifically the National Labor Relations Act (NLRA). The NLRA essentially guarantees the rights of employees (1) to organize, (2) to bargain collectively with their employers through a representative of their own choosing, (3) to engage in other concerted activities, or (4) to refrain from all such activity. The NLRA limits activities of employers and unions so that employees may exercise their statutory rights.

Even if your organization has no union representation, it's very likely that the NLRA covers your business. All businesses whose materials, products or services cross state lines and affect other businesses engaged in such activities are covered by the NLRA. Businesses not covered by the NLRA may be covered by state and local laws that mimic the NLRA in the rights granted to employees.

The NLRA is administered by the five-member National Labor Relations Board (NLRB). The Board decides cases involving charges of unfair labor practices, which are alleged violations of the NRLA by either employers or unions. The NLRB's General Counsel and staff investigate and prosecute cases and conduct elections to determine or decertify employee representatives.

The NLRB does not act on its own initiative. It processes only those charges of unfair labor practices and petitions for employee elections that may be filed with it at any of its offices around the country.

Most states have their own labor relations laws protecting public employees. Because private sector employees are within the jurisdiction of the federal labor law, most state legislation affecting private employees relates to individual employment protections, not collective rights.

However, many states do have "right-to-work" laws that prevent employees from being compelled to join a labor union in order to keep a job. States may also regulate "agency shop" arrangements, where unions are permitted to receive fees from nonmembers for the administrative costs of representing the nonmembers in contract negotiations and grievance arbitration. Also, some states have extended labor relations laws to employees who are not covered by federal law.

> *Only the rights of "employees" are protected under the National Labor Relations Act. This means that supervisors, forepersons, and other members of management are not "employees" as the labor relations laws use the term. Nor are independent contractors "employees." People in those classifications generally have no "labor rights."*

What is an unfair labor practice?

An "unfair labor practice" occurs when an employer interferes with rights protected by the NLRA or discriminates against employees who exercise these rights. (Unions can also be charged with unfair labor practices for violating the Act.) It is also unlawful for employers to interfere with, discriminate against, or retaliate against employees who bring complaints or file unfair labor practice charges.

What is concerted activity?

Beyond the right to unionize and bargain collectively through a union, federal labor law gives employees the right "to engage in other concerted activities for the purpose of collective bargaining or other mutual aid or protection." What does this mean?

The NLRA doesn't define "other concerted activities" but it has come to mean joint employee activities aimed at improving pay, benefits, or working conditions. For an action to be concerted, it must be aimed at improving conditions for more than one employee.

What is the difference between personal activity and concerted activity? Personal activity or actions taken solely for the benefit of one employee are not covered by the NLRA. But the distinction between personal and concerted activity is not always easy to see.

> **Example:** *If one employee pickets outside her employer's business to protest her suspension, her action is not concerted activity. However, if a group of her coworkers picket their employer protesting the first employee's suspension, that is protected activity even though the protest seems to be aimed as resolving one employee's concerns. The group's action is protected because the presumption is the employees are acting on the thought that the same unfair suspension could happen to them in the future, and their coworkers would help them.*

WHAT you need to know: Concerted activity doesn't require a group consensus as to the desired outcome of the action. Employees who complain as a group about working conditions may be protected even if they don't collectively agree on what actions they will take if their complaints are not addressed.

✓ Checklist

Is an employee's action personal or concerted activity? The answers to these questions will help determine whether the activity is protected by the NLRA.

- ☐ Are two or more employees acting as a group to complain about or rectify working conditions?
- ☐ Did the employee take part in the action with other employees?
- ☐ Did the employee act for reasons that were not strictly personal?
- ☐ Is the employee acting other than by and on behalf of himself or herself?
- ☐ Did the employee engage in the action on the authority of other employees?
- ☐ Did the employee's complaint arise out of a meeting or discussion with other employees?
- ☐ Has the employee been designated as a spokesperson by other employees?
- ☐ Are other employees aware of and interested in the outcome of the employee's actions?

What is protected activity?

Protected activity is conduct an employee is free to engage in without interference by an employer or restraint or coercion by a union. Keep in mind that not all concerted activity is protected activity. Even when employees take collective action aimed at mutual aid or protection, if the action is not undertaken for the purpose of improving terms or conditions of their employment, their action is not protected. Employee collective action must be job-related to be protected.

> ***Example:*** *A group of drivers sabotage a company delivery van. Although the drivers act as a group, their conduct is not protected by the NLRA because the conduct was not aimed at improving work conditions.*

All employees are allowed to engage in protected activities. Membership in a union is not required, and it does not matter if employees are acting through a union or not.

Employee actions considered concerted, protected activity

Assuming the following actions are undertaken for mutual aid and protection, and are related to improving working conditions, the following are examples of protected activities:
- talking to co-workers in person or on the telephone to urge them to support the union;
- sending email to co-workers;
- signing a petition;
- going as a group to talk to the supervisor or human resources office;
- sending one member of the group to talk to the supervisor or human resources office;
- staging a walkout or work stoppage;
- contacting employees of *other* employers to engage in a common cause; and
- filing an unfair labor practice charge or other complaint with a federal or state administrative agency (*even* if the charges prove to be false).

Remember Kent yelling expletives at his supervisor Harry? Verbal conduct is generally protected by the NLRA, even if that conduct is disruptive and inflammatory. Expletives and other coarse or rough speech are often shrugged off as "the language of the shop" and a natural but tolerable outgrowth of labor-management contention.

In a similar case, the NLRB ruled that an employee's profane outburst at a supervisor was protected conduct because the employee was provoked by the supervisor's overt hostility, which included a threat for engaging in protected activity. Before the outburst, there was no basis to find that the employee had engaged in inappropriate conduct in discussing the merits of his wage complaint.

Not all actions are protected by the NLRA

Egregious or outrageous actions are not protected by the NLRA, however. When an employee's act is overly derogatory, defamatory, malicious, or insubordinate, the law will not protect it from an employer's disciplinary action.

The NLRA is not meant to give cover to activity that interferes with production or undermines customer relationships. If the activity violates a statute, is accompanied by violence, or is carried out in defiance of an employer's property rights, it will not be protected by federal law.

Employer interference

What does interference mean? Interference is defined as the action (or nonaction) taken by employers that infringes on the rights of employees to join (or not join) together for the purpose of mutual aid or protection, or for collective bargaining. Charges of unlawful interference can arise not only from conduct during a union election campaign, but employers can be charged with interference with employees' protected rights even after the union is either fully entrenched or defeated.

> **Example 1:** A hospital's no-solicitation/no-distribution policy was unlawful interference because it restricted solicitation and distribution of employees and nonemployees in all areas of the hospital, including office buildings that were not attached to the hospital facility. The hospital did not show that its policy was necessary to avoid disrupting health care operations or disturbing patients.
>
> **Example 2:** Questioning employees about their knowledge of or support for a union, especially in a manner that makes employees feel the employer is keeping track of who supports the union, is unlawful interference.
>
> **Example 3:** Spying on union gatherings or conducting other surveillance or even creating the impression of surveillance is unlawful interference.
>
> **Example 4:** Threatening employees with job loss or other reprisal if they join or vote for a union is an obvious example of unlawful employer interference.

Union activities

Organizing campaigns

A union election typically begins with a union organizing drive. An organizing drive may occur after the union has sent out "feelers" to the employer it hopes to organize to ascertain the level of interest among employees. Alternatively, an employee or group of employees might contact a union and request information or assistance in gaining union representation or resolving a problem with their employer.

Either way, once this contact is made, the union will begin distributing materials to employees, meeting with employees to ascertain the degree of interest and the key issues causing dissatisfaction, and building a committee of employees to drive the campaign.

HR How-to: EMPLOYMENT LAW

Before a union election is held, the union and employer vigorously attempt to persuade the employees to vote to accept or reject the union. This campaign is similar in some ways to a political contest. Both sides carefully track their levels of support.

What an employer can do. Employers have cited a number of telltale signs that organizing activity has begun, such as: questions or grievances suddenly are being raised by a committee of employees rather than individual staff members; fliers appear on car windshields in employee parking lots; or employees become engaged in more frequent and more secretive discussions.

Employer can express opposition to union. The NLRA acknowledges that an employer has the right to express its opposition to a union. There are limits on the employer's opposition, however. It must not undermine employees' free choice by making statements aimed to threaten or intimidate them, or make promises that would induce them into voting against the union.

An employer cannot discriminate against employees who demonstrate their support for a union. This means that managers cannot discharge employees simply because of their organizing activities. However, an employer is not required to tolerate insubordination or poor work by an employee simply because he or she is a union activist. If an employer would discharge or discipline an employee even if he or she were not engaged in union activity, then the law allows an employer to do so.

An employer is required to maintain the status quo with regard to the terms and conditions of employment.

During a union organizing campaign, the law does not allow employers to suddenly grant pay increases or implement employee governance systems or grievance procedures. These morale improvement efforts will be seen as interference with employee choice.

However, if a pay increase was scheduled and employees reasonably expected the increase, then it cannot be withheld simply because of a union drive, as this too would be unlawful discrimination.

Unlawful interference during an election campaign is considered an "unfair labor practice." That's why it's important to ensure that your managers at all levels know the law and are trained in union avoidance within its parameters. The organization is legally liable for the unlawful actions committed by managers and supervisors during a union organizing campaign.

Best Practices

Train supervisors to avoid committing unfair labor practices
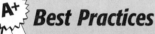

The likelihood of unfair labor practices occurring within an organization is greater when an organizing drive or contract negotiation is under way. Training and regular communication with managers and supervisors is critical during these periods. Urge your supervisors and managers to don a tough outer shell when the institution faces a contentious labor dispute.

Let them know you understand that they may want to take disciplinary action against an employee for disparaging management when talking to coworkers about the perceived benefits of a union contract. But remind them that the law allows considerable freedom to speak in this vein. Tell your supervisors and managers that any attempts to quash such speech, or to discipline the speakers, may well result in unfair labor practice charges and the liabilities that accompany them.

Because employees cannot be singled out for disciplinary action simply because they are union members or active union proponents, supervisors must carefully build and preserve a record of infractions to support action taken against an employee who is unproductive or engages in misconduct. This is especially true when the employee is a union activist. Before a supervisor discharges or disciplines an employee, the manager should examine not only the immediate justification for the termination but also consider prior circumstances that may continue to shield the employee from discharge.

For example, a lone employee who engages in concerted activity when making an individual complaint regarding a subject that he has complained about jointly with other employees in the past is engaging in protected activity because the complaint will be considered a continuation of the prior concerted action. Remember, the context in which employee activities *and* disciplinary actions take place is the primary determinant of whether the activities or the disciplinary measures imposed are lawful.

✓ Checklist

Employer dos and don'ts of communication

Employers have a free speech right to communicate with employees about their opposition to the union. However, there are limits to this right. Employers lawfully may:

- [ ] offer an opinion that joining a union may result in income loss due to strikes, initiation fees, and dues;
- [ ] recount what happened in other companies when employees selected a union to represent them, such as a strike or a plant closing;
- [ ] tell employees how their wages, benefits, and working conditions compare with those offered at other companies;
- [ ] reveal to employees any untrue statements the union may have made in various campaign materials;
- [ ] relay management's position that it would prefer to communicate directly with employees rather than through a union;
- [ ] explain that a union cannot require an employer to do anything it chooses not to do. An employer will not be required to agree to any union demands during bargaining.

Employers may not:

- [ ] question employees about their union activities or membership (in such circumstances that would tend to restrain or coerce the employees, or make them feel as though they are being watched);

- ☐ ask employees about how they intend to vote (or voted) in the election;
- ☐ spy on union gatherings or conduct other surveillance;
- ☐ use spies, informers, or supervisors to monitor union activities or create the *impression* of surveillance;
- ☐ provide benefits (such as wage increases) deliberately timed to influence voting and discourage employees from forming a union;
- ☐ withhold benefits (such as a scheduled wage increases) to discourage employees to vote for a union;
- ☐ threaten to close the business or plant if the union is elected;
- ☐ threaten employees with loss of jobs or other reprisals if they join or vote for the union;
- ☐ threaten with or actually use physical force to influence votes;
- ☐ discipline, discharge, or take other reprisals against employees who support the union;
- ☐ incite racial, ethnic, or religious prejudice through the use of inflammatory campaign appeals.

Easy reminder for supervisors and managers. When communicating with supervisory personnel and other managers about union activities, these restrictions can be simplified into a useful acronym. Remind supervisors and managers of the following **TIPS** of what to avoid during a union organizing campaign:

Threats

Interrogation

Promises (of benefits for voting against a union)

Surveillance

What happens in a union election?

The first step for a union in seeking an election to demonstrate that it has the right to represent certain employees is to file a petition with the National Labor Relations Board (NLRB). The petition identifies the employer and the petitioning union, and the size and form of the bargaining unit that it proposes.

Within 48 hours of filing the petition, the union must provide evidence of support among bargaining unit employees in order to obtain a representation election.

The union is not required to show that it has the support of a majority of employees. Rather, the union need only show that 30 percent of the employees in a potential bargaining unit support the union.

A union usually demonstrates such support by presenting signed "authorization cards" to the NLRB. Authorization cards are documents signed by employees indicating that they authorize the union to act as their collective bargaining representative.

After the petition is filed, the local regional office of the NLRB will investigate the petition and determine whether the union and the employer are covered by the NLRA.

The Board also decides whether the proposed bargaining unit is appropriate. The Board will then attempt to resolve, with the consent of the union and employer, such issues as which employees are eligible to vote and when the election will be held. A representation election occurs by secret ballot, usually at the employer's workplace during work hours. The election is supervised by the NLRB and the ballots counted.

A union wins a representation election if a majority of ballots cast by eligible employees within a potential bargaining unit indicate that the employees want the union to serve as their exclusive bargaining representative.

*A union does not win an election that results in a tie—to be the exclusive bargaining representative, a union must have **majority** support.*

Union membership is dropping

The percentage of union-organized workers in the United States is at its lowest level in decades at 13.2 percent, according to 2003 US Department of Labor's Bureau of Labor Statistics. The union membership rate has steadily declined from a high of 20.1 percent in 1983, the first year comparable union data was available.

While there many be many reasons why unions represent only 13.2 percent of the workforce, unions still represent millions of employees, as well as millions of dollars in dues money and billions of dollars in pension contributions.

Why some employees are attracted to unions. Businesses often wonder why employees would want to be represented by a union. According to industrial relations practitioners, there are generally four reasons why a worker would want to unionize. They are:
1. poor, unsafe, or unhealthy working conditions;
2. a perceived lack of job security;
3. inadequate wages and benefits; and
4. a need for more control over work life.

While the first three reasons may be easily understandable, they are also readily correctable within reason. However, the fourth factor is harder to understand, harder yet to neutralize, and impossible to completely avoid. Nevertheless, it is perhaps the strongest motivation for unionization today.

> The major elements of dissatisfaction among the workforce relate to job content rather than terms of employment. While workers may desire to be creative, assume responsibility, and exercise control over the job environment, often the job is performed under conditions that require work utterly lacking in mobility, interest, challenge, change or autonomy of decision.

Best Practices
Preventive strategies to deter employees from contacting a union

The best way to deter employees from contacting a union? The simple answer is to keep employees happy. Of course, the answer is far less simple in practice. This reality underscores the critical role that human resources professionals play in union avoidance. As the professionals responsible for managing employee relations and the challenging task of optimizing employee satisfaction, HR's proactive participation is essential. These steps should be taken well before a dissatisfied employee contacts a union:

Assess your organization's vulnerability. Do you know the biggest work-related concerns facing your staff? What is the organization's current retention rate? Are there "problem" managers as reflected by high turnover in particular units? Are pay and benefits in keeping with area standards? Identify patterns of employee turnover, key issues affecting employee satisfaction, and managerial weaknesses that demand attention.

Communicate with employees. Ongoing communication with employees is the most effective union avoidance strategy that an employer can adopt. Having assessed the areas of vulnerability, a well-executed communications strategy can address them. Be ready to answer to known vulnerabilities head-on. Frame employer responses to key employee concerns in advance, and be on alert to shape a well-crafted message when unexpected issues arise. Keep employees informed of business decisions made—even those decisions they will perceive as negative. Proactive communication cannot just occur on occasion. Such efforts must be integrated into the organization's culture.

Train your managers and supervisors. An aggressive management training and leadership development program is essential to ensure that supervisors and managers are prepared for their roles. Supervisors and managers must be trained in union avoidance and compliance with labor law.

Poorly prepared managers who react improperly to organizing activity can incur legal liability for the organization and also galvanize support for the union.

Involve employees in decision-making. Broaden employee participation in management. Employee involvement committees yield a share of decision-making to staff who may justly feel that they have particular expertise in certain areas or functions within the organization. Shared power gives employees a voice as well as an understanding of the constraints faced by management as they strive to balance the sometimes conflicting interests in employee satisfaction and the institution's fiscal well-being.

Provide space for grievances. An important element of employees' satisfaction is the sense that they are being treated fairly. Consistent, fairly administered disciplinary procedures can help lessen the employer's vulnerability to employee lawsuits—and to a unionization drive.

Remedy the issues. Respond to employee grievances with specific outcomes wherever possible. For example, award reasonable merit increases if economically feasible, and if not, explain why budgetary constraints simply will not allow for the added labor costs. Employees should see no benefits to union representation that the employer cannot directly provide itself—without having to pay union dues.

A word of caution. The NLRA does not allow an employer to "fix what's broken" once a union organizing campaign is underway. The law carries a presumption that attempts to resolve grievances or meet employee demands at this time are aimed to sway a workforce to vote against the union. The law considers such efforts to be interference with employee free choice. Thus, for reasons both legal and practical, the time to initiate a communications strategy, organize employee involvement committees, implement a grievance procedure, and solicit and remedy employee concerns is *before* a union organizer comes knocking.

The employee handbook

The employee handbook is an essential communication tool and a key element of a preventive employee relations program. The handbook provides an introduction to the company, a uniform source of employer policies and employee benefits, and a common core of information for all employees. Handbooks eliminate uncertainty about company policies and benefits and reduce the risk they will be administered inconsistently. For that reason, even small companies will benefit from having a current and comprehensive employee handbook.

Writing or updating the handbook

When drafting an employee handbook, HR, together with management representatives, should review all existing written policies and manuals as well as any unwritten practices.

Inconsistencies and inadequacies should be examined and corrected as part of the process.

Clarity and consistency in language and form are critical in drafting the handbook.
- The handbook language should create a positive perception of the company.
- The contents should be arranged in an orderly and logical fashion with topical headings and subheadings to facilitate reference to particular policies.
- Sentences should be kept short and overall writing style simple.
- Avoid ambiguous or complex terminology.
- Each policy should be clear and concise.
- A table of contents and/or index should be included.

While every handbook must be tailored to the needs of the company and to the specific requirements of state and local laws, typical provisions include the following:
- **Letter of welcome from the Chief Executive Officer.** Since most employees are interested in learning about the company's origins and founders, the letter might include a short statement about the history of the company.

◆ **Company position on employee relations and unions.** The handbook might include a statement summarizing the employer's philosophy regarding employee relations and unions.

> ***Example:*** *Our success is founded on the skill and efforts of our employees. Our policy is to deal with our employees honestly and to respect and recognize them as individuals. In our opinion, unionization would interfere with the individual treatment, respect, and recognition we value.*

◆ **Problem-solving procedures.** The handbook should also describe the company's philosophy and procedures for the resolution of employee problems, such as an "open door" policy or an alternative dispute resolution procedure.
◆ **Receipt and disclaimer.** Each employee should sign an appropriate receipt for the handbook, including a disclaimer acknowledging that the handbook does not constitute a contract of employment. This receipt should be a separate tear-out page, kept in the employee's personnel file. If the handbook contains a union-free policy statement, it should be separate from the receipt. The receipt should not condition employment on adherence to the employer's policies, which by implication would include opposition to unionization.

> In a union setting, an employer should be cautious about inserting a union-free statement in an employee handbook. In one case, the NLRB ruled that issuing a handbook with a union-free policy, along with a statement of acknowledgement that employees agreed to be bound by handbook policies, was a violation of the NLRA because the statement suggested coercion of employees to refrain from organizing.

Avoiding litigation

A carelessly written handbook can be a minefield of legal problems for the employer. In recent years, the content of employee handbooks increasingly has become the subject of litigation. Employees often claim that handbook statements create contractual obligations that the employer has failed to meet.

Properly drafted employee manuals can reduce the likelihood of costly and time-consuming litigation.

The courts of some states have recognized that personnel policy handbooks may form the basis of an implied contract between employer and employee in the absence of a clear disclaimer stating that the handbook does not constitute a contract. As noted earlier, a disclaimer should be included stating explicitly that "the handbook and the policies therein do not constitute a contract."

If your employee handbook provides for arbitration as an alternative dispute resolution procedure, the receipt should cross-reference the agreement to arbitrate; for example, "I hereby agree to arbitrate employment disputes as set forth in the handbook." The disclaimer should be conspicuous and highlighted with bold, capital, larger typeface, or italics.

Handbook terminology

Terminology common to personnel policy handbooks can also result in wrongful discharge litigation. For example, many handbooks refer to "probationary employees" who are subject to termination for any reason during the initial period of employment. This may imply, however, that employees who have passed their probationary period have some kind of job guarantee.

To avoid the implication that employment becomes permanent and is no longer "at will," employers may wish to designate the period immediately following an employee's commencement of work as an "introductory period" and refer to workers who have completed their introductory period as "regular" employees, not "permanent."

It is important that the term "employment at will" be defined. If not, depending on the state, a jury may decide whether the employee knew or should have known what it means to be employed "at will." A simple explanation is that the company is free to terminate employees at any time for any reason, just as employees are free to terminate their employment at any time for any reason.

Care should be taken in dealing with another aspect of job security. Employers should avoid promising that an employee will not be discharged except for "just cause," because if they do, they may end up litigating exactly what "just cause" means. Remember, an employer has the right to set its own standards for employees. A failure to meet such standards constitutes cause for dismissal.

Legal and human resources issues have become intertwined; nowhere is this more true than with employee handbooks. Since employment laws vary from state to state, it's always a good idea for HR professionals to consult with employment counsel when developing the handbook.

The Quiz

1. The NLRA guarantees employees the right to organize and to bargain collectively with their employers. ☐ True ☐ False

2. If a group of employees is talking with a supervisor about improving working conditions, this is a protected activity. ☐ True ☐ False

3. Once a union organizing campaign starts, an employer can:
   (a) Express opposition to a union.
   (b) Tell employees they'll be fired if a union is approved.
   (c) Withhold a scheduled pay increase.
   (d) All of the above.
   (e) None of the above.

4. Clarity and consistency are important elements of an employee handbook. ☐ True ☐ False

Answer key: 1. T; 2. T; 3. a; 4. T

Chapter 10

Termination

Terminating an employee **216**
    BEST PRACTICES: Do complete investigation
    and document it **217**
How to terminate **217**
Terminating groups of employees **220**
Conducting a termination meeting **223**
Voluntary resignations **228**
Prompted resignations **229**
Exit interviews **231**
The Quiz **236**

> Cassie is a senior engineer who has been working for your company for twelve years. Formerly an "outstanding" performer, her performance has slipped significantly in the last year. She's missed deadlines and turned in substandard work. You've talked with her several times, put her on probation, and put her in a performance improvement program. Cassie's supervisor has just told you that she's just turned in an incomplete project. He's tired of spending so much time correcting her substandard work and wants to fire her at the end of today's shift. Should you tell him to go ahead?

Terminating an employee

Firing someone is a task most people would rather avoid. No matter the reason for the termination, confronting an employee and telling him or her of the termination is a difficult job, even if the termination is justified.

There are legitimate reasons for terminating an employee, including repeated poor performance, misconduct, or a dismissal during a reduction in force. There are also reasons for which an employee should never be terminated, such as whistleblowing, union activity, and retaliation. Whatever the reason, an employee should never be fired on the spot. Firing an employee on the spot can get a company into trouble. Stress to your supervisors and managers that every termination decision should be carefully reviewed for fairness, legality and consistency with company policy.

The less care that is given to making a decision to fire someone, the greater risk the company will wind up in court.

Suspension during investigation. Even if an employee has committed a serious offense that clearly calls for termination, it is often better to suspend the employee than to immediately fire him or her. The employee should be told of the suspension and asked to leave the premises until further contact from management. An investigation of the surrounding circumstances may uncover facts that explain the employee's behavior or make termination inappropriate.

Remember Cassie? Although you've worked with her during the past year to improve her performance, firing her on the spot could be a big mistake. Has Cassie been told her poor performance could lead to job termination? Have you adequately investigated to find out the reason for the deterioration of her performance? Is she working with new equipment but has not been trained or had inadequate training? What are her work conditions like? Is she being harassed? Does she have a disability? If so, does she need an accommodation? Has she requested an accommodation that isn't working? As you can see, there are many questions that must be answered even in situations that appear "obvious." Telling her supervisor to "go ahead" before investigating more would be wrong.

> **Best Practices**
>
> **Do complete investigation and document it**
>
> Two employees, Kevin and Ahmad, had a long-standing fractious relationship that escalated into a shouting match in the cafeteria during their lunch break. Kevin walked out of the cafeteria and into the hallway, followed by Ahmad who was still shouting. Kevin pushed Ahmad into the wall and punched him several times before walking away. Ahmad ran after Kevin and hit him in the back and head. The fight continued until broken up by coworkers.
>
> Upon learning of the fight, the supervisor suspended both men pending an investigation. After the investigation, the supervisor determined the men were equally responsible and fired them both. They sued the employer for wrongful discharge.
>
> In a court decision based on similar facts, the employer was able to show the court that a thorough investigation was made into the fight, including the interviewing of witnesses and viewing of a security tape, which had taped the fight. Each man was given the chance to tell his side of the story during the investigation. Also, both men admitted knowing that they could be fired for fighting and acknowledged their signatures on a copy of the company work rules which plainly stated "employees may be fired for fighting on company premises." The employer followed best practice here, by not rushing to judgement. Instead, it did a complete investigation, which it documented, and that saved the day in court.

How to terminate

Employers would probably find it much easier if all that had to be done was say "you're fired!" to end an employment relationship—but that's not the way it is. Any termination could lead to a quagmire of problems for an employer, so to lessen the possibility of fallout from legal action, check and recheck all actions taken prior to an employee's termination. Below are guidelines for you to follow.

Make sure the investigation was complete. A complete investigation includes gathering and completing a written report of all the facts and written witness statements; preserving physical evidence and records; reviewing all personnel records, including disciplinary records; and comparing actions in similar situations.

Prove that the termination was fair and followed company policies and practices. In addition to a company being held to its own rules, a company may be called upon to "prove" the events were true. Is there documentation to prove that the events were true and that company policies and procedures were followed?

Review the documentation. Double-check any facts cited in your paperwork. Make sure there are proper authorizations for all actions taken. Determine whether the proper forms have been used.

✓ Checklist

Questions to ask during the investigation—before termination

- ☐ What specific company policy or work rule violation authorizes the termination?
- ☐ Where is the rule written?
- ☐ Is the rule reasonably related to the orderly, efficient and safe operation of the company?
- ☐ Does the rule require conduct that can reasonably expected of the employee?
- ☐ How do you know that the employee knew the behavior was against company rules?
- ☐ Has the employee had an opportunity to present his or her side of the story?
- ☐ Was there an investigation to determine whether the employee actually engaged in conduct that violated the rule?
- ☐ Was the investigation of the conduct fair and objective?
- ☐ Did the investigation attempt to find out the employee's version of events?

Chapter 10—Termination 219

> - ☐ Did the investigation find enough facts to show that the employee acted improperly?
> - ☐ Did the employee have an opportunity to make necessary changes in behavior?
> - ☐ Is termination appropriate for this infraction?
> - ☐ Have procedures in the company's progressive discipline policy been followed?
> - ☐ If the employee is covered by a union contract, have disciplinary procedures set forth in the contract been followed?
> - ☐ Is the termination consistent with punishment in other similar situations?

A review should also be conducted to ensure that an employee is not being terminated because he or she belongs to a protected category. A "yes" answer to any of the questions below is a warning sign that the planned termination may be illegal. Further investigation should be done before proceeding with the termination.

✓ Checklist
**Checklist
Legality review**

> - ☐ Could any of the following protected categories be a factor in the recommendation to terminate employees?
>   - ☐ Race or color
>   - ☐ Religion
>   - ☐ Sex
>   - ☐ Age
>   - ☐ Disability
>   - ☐ National origin
>   - ☐ Citizenship status
>   - ☐ Veteran or military status
>   - ☐ Arrest records
>   - ☐ Marital status
>   - ☐ Sexual orientation
>   - ☐ State of residency
>   - ☐ Political affiliation
>   - ☐ Lawful off-duty activities
>
> *Continued on next page*

Continued from previous page

- ☐ Could the discharge have the appearance of discriminating on the basis of one of the above protected categories?
- ☐ Has the employee complained of abuse or harassment?
- ☐ Is there any reason to believe the employee may have a disability that has impaired his or her work performance?
- ☐ Has a request by the employee for a disability or religious accommodation been refused?
- ☐ Has the employee had medical treatment recently?
- ☐ Is the employee pregnant?
- ☐ Has the employee applied for or returned from a medically related leave of absence recently?
- ☐ Has the employee recently requested a military leave?
- ☐ Has the employee recently returned from a military leave?
- ☐ Has the employee engaged in union activities?
- ☐ Has the employee been promised any terms or conditions of employment by anyone in a position of authority?
- ☐ Is the employee about to vest in any benefit?
- ☐ Are the employee's wages being attached or garnished?
- ☐ Has the employee complained about wages, hours, or other work conditions?
- ☐ Has the employee reported company wrongdoing?
- ☐ Did the employee refuse to do an action because it was against the law?
- ☐ Has the employee filed a grievance or complaint against the company?
- ☐ Has the employee filed a workers' compensation claim?

Terminating groups of employees

Reductions in force, layoffs, downsizing, rightsizing, and reengineering are terms that have come to mean, in certain circumstances, the same thing—involuntary loss of jobs without regard to individual performance for groups of employees. Except for layoffs, these involve a permanent severance of the employment relationship. Generally, "layoff" means a temporary loss of jobs, usually in a unionized workplace.

When you terminate an employee, there are many potential compliance issues. The range of issues is greatly increased when groups of employees are terminated for no cause on their part.

Most of the legal challenges that occur arise from:
- charges of age, race or sex discrimination;
- claims brought under the Americans with Disabilities Act;
- lawsuits alleging both written and oral breach of contract;
- unfair labor practice complaints filed by union workers; and
- claims under Employee Retirement Income Security Act (ERISA) or Consolidated Omnibus Budget Reconciliation Act of 1985 (COBRA)

Worker Adjustment and Retraining Notification Act. Complaints also arise that proper notice and timing under the Worker Adjustment and Retraining Notification Act (WARN) were not followed. WARN is a federal law that requires 60 days advance written notice of plant closings and mass layoffs for employers of 100 or more fulltime employees or 100 or more employees who work a total of 4,000 hours per week excluding overtime. The law applies to situations when a single site suffers an employment loss that affects at least 33% of the site's fulltime workforce and 50 or more fulltime workers at that site during any 30-day period.

In addition to issuing notice at least 60 days prior to the implementation of a mass layoff or plant closing, employers must fulfill certain notice requirements.

Who must receive notice? In a nonunion setting, notice must be given to all "affected employees." In a union setting, notice must be given to the union. The notice should be addressed to the chief elected officer of the union. If this person is not the same as the officer of each local union, the Department of Labor recommends that notice also be given to the local union officials.

In union and nonunion settings, notice must be given to the state dislocated worker unit, or, if this unit has not been set up, to the governor of the state.

Additionally, notice must be given to the local political unit in union and nonunion settings. The notice is to be addressed to the highest ranking official or the chairperson of a board or committee. If there is more than one local jurisdiction, notice goes to the one to which the employer pays the most taxes, combining all taxes together.

Penalties. Employers that violate the WARN Act can be required to make payment of back pay and benefits to each employee, and a fine of not more than $500 per day.

Exceptions. Less than 60 days notice may be given under three exceptions: (1) faltering company, (2) unforeseeable business circumstances, and (3) natural disasters. Employers have the burden of proving the conditions and must give as much notice as practicable. If notice is given, employers must include a brief statement explaining why a full 60-day notice was not given.

Demographic mix. Be careful and ensure that the group that is downsized is a reflection of the demographic mix of your workforce. If not, you must be prepared to explain why the mix of terminated employees is different and that the difference is in no way discriminatory.

You cannot use a reduction in force to eliminate individuals' jobs arbitrarily because you will face potential litigation. If you use a merit system, then you can eliminate the positions of employees whose performance has been documented as less than satisfactory. If there is no documentation, then you cannot eliminate the person's position without possible liability.

In this process you do not want to "cut corners." A reduction in force is one of the most common actions that generates legal challenges. You should be careful to follow your policies to the letter.

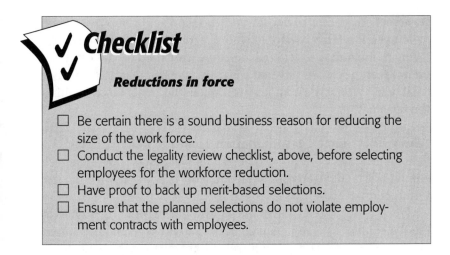

Checklist

Reductions in force

- ☐ Be certain there is a sound business reason for reducing the size of the work force.
- ☐ Conduct the legality review checklist, above, before selecting employees for the workforce reduction.
- ☐ Have proof to back up merit-based selections.
- ☐ Ensure that the planned selections do not violate employment contracts with employees.

Conducting a termination meeting

So the decision has been made to terminate an employee. Because termination is such an unpleasant and stressful task, you'll want to carefully plan what the termination meeting should accomplish. Careful planning will ensure that the termination meeting efficiently communicates to the employee the termination decision and the reason for the decision.

The meeting should be conducted in a manner that maintains the dignity of the person being terminated. Also, the reputation of the company as an employer that deals fairly with its people should be maintained.

The termination meeting is the last opportunity a company has to decrease the likelihood that an employee will file a lawsuit challenging the termination.

To decrease potential liability, the termination meeting should be conducted in a manner that:

- ♦ maintains the dignity of the person being fired and minimized as much as possible the resentment the discharged person feels toward the company; and
- ♦ explains the reason for the discharge.

Be direct. According to one lawyer who represents employees who have been fired, many people who sue for wrongful discharge are trying to find out the "real reason" they were fired or laid off. They do not feel they were "leveled with" by management and seek out legal help to force the company to explain the "real reason" behind the termination.

Who will conduct the termination meeting? In most cases, the immediate supervisor or superior should be responsible. The task should not be delegated to someone who was not involved in the termination decision.

Ideally, supervisors and managers should be properly trained to handle conflict as a key management skill. However, not all supervisors are trained and, even if trained, many are not comfortable handling conflict. Since there is significant liability to the employer, a supervisor who feels uncomfortable should not be forced to conduct the meeting without support. If a supervisor needs additional support, consider one or all of the following:

- Role playing with another supervisor after preparing for the meeting. Have a third person critique the play.
- Rehearse key parts of the termination meeting in front of a mirror or a video camera
- Advise the supervisor that it is better to say "I do not know but will find out and let you know by (specific date)," than to answer a question incorrectly or not answer a legitimate question.

It is also to the company's advantage if you, as the human resources professional, sits in on the meeting.

What if the employee requests a witness? It is probably best to allow this so that the employee does not feel he or she is being railroaded out the door unfairly. It should be explained, however, that the witness is there only to observe the meeting, not to act as a representative for the employee's side.

If the employee is represented by a union, a request for a representative does not have to be granted if the purpose of the meeting is merely to inform the person of an irrevocable decision to discharge that has previously been made.

Management may want a third person present if trouble is expected or if an objective third person is needed. A second management representative may be seen, however, as an attempt to gang up on the terminated employee.

Where should the meeting be held? The meeting should be held privately at a neutral site other than the manager's office. The room should be a place with a working telephone and, preferably, at least one wall of uncovered glass. The room should also be a well-lit area with at least two chairs and a desk.

When should the meeting be held? Early in the day and early in the week is the best time for conducting a termination interview. People are more relaxed, more rested, and better equipped to handle stress earlier in the day. People tend to be tired and short-tempered later in the day, and this may increase the chance for an unpleasant reaction to bad news.

> Other tips on when to hold the meeting:
>
> **Avoid Friday.** An employee who is fired on Friday has two days to brood about his or her treatment by the company.
>
> **Avoid holidays and vacations.** Do not schedule the meeting on the last working day of the workweek or before a holiday vacation.
>
> **Meet face-to-face.** The discharge decision should be communicated face-to-face, never by letter, "pink slip" or over the phone.

What to do during the termination meeting. The actual meeting to inform an employee that he or she is being terminated should take about ten minutes. The purpose is to communicate that a decision has been made to terminate the employee and the reasons behind that decision. Use the following checklist for conducting the termination meeting.

✓ Checklist
Conducting the meeting

- [ ] Emphasize that the decision is final and irreversible, all relevant factors were reviewed, and there is agreement at all management levels.
- [ ] Display empathy for the employee's situation but do not sympathize or become a friend to the person. If the person starts to cry, allow the expression of emotion to occur and just offer some tissue. Avoid trying to soften the bad news.
- [ ] Don't hold out any hope that the decision will be changed or that there is a possibility for any kind of bargaining.
- [ ] Don't "blame" the decision on upper management. Avoid making statements such as "They decided to terminate your employment." Remember, you must communicate that there is agreement on the decision at all levels of management.
- [ ] Don't lose control of the meeting or stray from the central issue of informing the person of a predetermined result. Be firm and honest, but allow the person to have his or her say. Don't interrupt or talk over the person if he or she maintains a business-like tone. If the person tries to argue with the decision, react by saying words such as "I understand what you are saying, but the decision stands and will not be changed." If the employee becomes angry or abusive, do not respond in a similar manner. Maintain a normal tone of voice. State firmly that the meeting will not continue under such conditions.
- [ ] Don't respond to a threat to file a lawsuit. That is the right of any person.
- [ ] Don't discuss the situation of any other employee.
- [ ] Communicate the reasons for the termination in factual terms. Do not make value judgments about the person's character or work ethic.
- [ ] End the meeting by telling the person the effective date of the termination and the manner in which he or she is to leave the premises. Inform the person about final payment and benefits.

How to start the meeting. The first moments of the termination session will often dictate the tone for the rest of the meeting. This is when to establish control of the meeting. An opening statement should be thought out and rehearsed. The statement should first inform the employee that a termination decision has been made, followed by the reason for the termination. The tone of the statement should be non-judgmental. Words should be chosen that do not provoke a hostile reaction or invite an argument about the merits of the decision.

> *Example 1: Poor Performance*—*Jim, we have decided to end your employment with the company. As you recall, we tried several times in counseling sessions to warn you that your performance needed to improve. In the last meeting held on (date) you were specifically told that failure to improve your productivity and work quality to acceptable levels could lead to termination. Unfortunately, you were unable to achieve the performance goals set out in that meeting. That inability to meet acceptable performance goals after repeated counseling and warnings is the reason we have decided to take this action. Today is your last day of employment with the company.*
>
> *Example 2: Attendance Problems*—*Alice, I must advise you that your employment with the company is being ended effective today. We have decided to terminate your employment because of your absence and tardiness problems. You recall that we have discussed your attendance record several times in the last six months. In the written warning I gave you on (date) you were specifically informed that if you missed one more work day in a one-month period you would be terminated. Yesterday you did not show up for work and did not call to make arrangements to make up the time. I have no alternative but to follow through on the warning and terminate your employment.*

Here are more tips for the meeting:

- avoid statements that might indicate that you distrust the employee;
- do not allow yourself to become emotional;
- do not attempt to keep the employee from walking out of the meeting;
- do not touch the employee; and
- do not make any discriminatory or negative comments.

As part of your preparation for a termination meeting, be sure to list all of the company-owned items or materials you need to get from the employee. Remember, conducting a termination meeting can be stressful, so planning ahead will ensure you reacquire the desired company property.

When firing an employee, be sure to confiscate and/or deactivate any company-owned property including:

- *credit cards*
- *cell phones*
- *keys*
- *automobiles*
- *identification passes*
- *computer access*
- *pagers*
- *building entry passes*
- *laptops*

Voluntary resignations

There are instances where employees will voluntarily leave an employer, including acceptance of another job offer, change in career, return to school, or retirement. You should maintain a record of the reason an individual voluntarily resigns because:

- in the event of a legal challenge, you may need the information to prepare a defense;
- you might have to compare your past record with the action in question; and
- you need to know why employees are leaving your company, as turnover can be costly. High turnover is a particular unit may signal a bigger problem.

- You must analyze turnover for certain government-mandated reports, such as affirmative action plans.
- You can ensure that proper notices and information are given to resigning employees.

✓ Checklist

Voluntary resignations

- [ ] Determine whether the employee has provided advance notice of resignation as required by company policy.
- [ ] Find out why the employee is leaving.
- [ ] If the employee has chosen to resign instead of being fired, make sure that the choice is the employee's alone and that no one has pressured the employee to resign. Also determine whether company policy permits resignations instead of firing in the circumstances of the employee's case.
- [ ] Find out whether the employee is resigning in order to escape illegal or intolerable employment practices or conditions.
- [ ] Request that the resignation be in writing, that the reasons for resigning be stated, and that the employee sign the statement.
- [ ] Document the reason(s) why the employee resigned.

Prompted resignations

A prompted resignation is a resignation that appears to be voluntary on the surface. However, the idea or motivation for the resignation was instigated by someone else, usually a supervisor. Or the employee wishes to resign instead of being terminated.

> **Example:** *A university employer offers a non-tenured professor the choice of resigning or being fired after sexual harassment charges were filed against him by three students.*

Allowing an employee to resign instead of being fired and allowing supervisors to "negotiate" the terms and conditions of an employee's separation from the company are transactions that have unequal risks for an employer.

Generally, if an employer "treats" the prompted resignation as if it were a firing for all internal purposes, there is no greater risk to the employer by allowing the employee to resign. There may be some good will generated by allowing the employee to exit with a greater degree of dignity.

Guidelines for managing prompted resignations include:
- Ensure that the desire to resign and not be terminated is the employee's wish, and he or she has not been pressured by any company representative to resign.
- Do not try to encourage an employee to resign. Your pressure may be interpreted as coercion.
- Do not assume that the company has diminished potential liability from a prompted resignation as opposed to the employee being fired.

Allowing employees to resign. Employees who are allowed to resign may be less angry and not as quick to litigate. However, the courts will not refuse to consider the charges simply because the termination was, in form, a voluntary matter.

Ensure your company has a policy concerning prompted resignations. The policy should include under what circumstances an employee would be allowed to resign instead of being fired, who can approve that action and what the employment reference will say.

Maintain a separate category to record and track prompted resignations. The analysis of prompted resignations should be reported under the overall category of involuntary terminations and not under voluntary resignations.

What you can do to control prompted resignations. Control who can agree to a prompted resignation. Generally, two levels of management and an HR representative should approve the decision.

Don't give supervisors the "power and authority" to pressure employees into resigning to avoid having to justify firing the employee. Allowing such behavior gives the supervisor absolute power and places the company in extreme risk with no review or approval before the fact. To guard against this practice, a company can take the following steps.

- ◆ Request voluntary resignations be in writing, the reasons for the resignation be stated and the statement be signed by the employee. Follow-up directly with the former employee in any situation that deviates from this norm.
- ◆ Conduct exit interviews and follow-up by mail, if necessary, with employees who do not attend formal exit interviews.
- ◆ Train all supervisors and managers as to what they can and cannot do in certain situations.
- ◆ Require a supervisor's superior to review all voluntary resignations in their work units. Personal interviews with each employee should be part of the review.
- ◆ Ensure that all levels of management realize that unemployment costs are not avoided by pressuring an individual into resigning.
- ◆ Do not have policies and practices that penalize supervisors who "fire" a disproportionate number of employees in his or her work unit. Ensure that supervisors are penalized based on improper management techniques, and not by merely exceeding an arbitrary criteria.
- ◆ Protect the employee's dignity. Employees sue when they feel they have been treated wrongly and not necessarily when laws have been violated. Encouraging an atmosphere of respect for an employee is always a good policy.

Exit interviews

It is reasonable for an employer and for the resigning employee to have a mutual interest in following your exit procedure. Employers wish to know why employees leave and employees usually have questions concerning benefits, records and references. When exit interviews are routine and not perceived as threatening or coercive, the information exchanged can be extremely valid.

How should an exit interview be conducted? Do you want to ask employees why they are leaving? Do you want them to tell you what they liked and disliked about their jobs? Do you want to hear their suggestions on what might benefit employees still with you?

Not every employer wants the answer to these questions. In some situations, high turnover is expected and management knows and fully understands why people come and go. Often, though, the assumed reasons for turnover may be wrong. The employer who uses exit interviews usually does so in order to get employees' point of view at a point when the employee may be the most candid.

You may be able to use the information collected to identify strategies that may reduce employee turnover. You may also discover situations that need correcting or changing.

Conduct exit interviews to:

♦ *find out the real reason why individuals leave;*
♦ *give the company a final opportunity to preserve the relationship, if a person has resigned for reasons that are unfounded;*
♦ *provide an opportunity to explain any issues or answer any questions;*
♦ *promote a more positive feeling on the part of the departing employee; and*
♦ *provide information that will save money or improve working conditions in the future.*

Advantages of exit interviews. Through the exit interview process, employees can provide their honest thoughts about the company and what aspects of their tenure may have caused them to leave.

Among the advantages of having uniformly implemented exit interview procedures is that managers and HR personnel can get at the real reason why employees wish to leave the company and, in some cases, valuable employees could even be persuaded to stay if their concerns and reservations are discussed and considered and the sources of their dissatisfaction addressed in a timely manner. In addition, exit interviews help establish good relations with the employee as he or she walks out the door thus ensuring that the separation from employment is not a bitter affair, and both the employee and management can speak well of each other in the future.

Chapter 10—Termination 233

Consider the following if planning on establishing or improving your exit interview process.

> ### ✓ Checklist
> **The exit interview process**
>
> ☐ Schedule the interview early in the week of the employee's departure, never on the last day.
> ☐ The interview should be conducted in a private office so the employee can speak freely without fear of being overheard.
> ☐ If possible, make an appointment in advance to allow for preparation by the interviewer.
> ☐ Make sure that interviewer has reviewed past performance appraisals on the employee prior to the interview.
> ☐ If possible, have the interviewer meet with the employee's immediate supervisor to discuss any potential reasons why the employee is leaving.
> ☐ The interview should be conducted in a friendly manner.
> ☐ The employee must be given every opportunity to express the reasons for leaving.
> ☐ The interviewer should be prepared to discuss what measures, if any, can be taken to change the employee's mind (if the separation is voluntary).
> ☐ The interview should not last more than 30 minutes.

Requesting an exit interview. There are several ways in which an employer can request an exit interview.

> ***Example 1:*** *Hospital A requires an exit interview with each resigning employee and explains why it wants the interview. The hospital assures employees that what they say will not be held against them in any way.*

Example 2: *Manufacturer Q uses an "exit interview report" that has spaces at the top for the employee's name and address, date of hire, job title, current grade and salary, date of termination and the name of the supervisor the employee reports to. Then the form has space for comments on three items: (1) reason for leaving; (2) attitude toward job, and (3) attitude toward supervisor. Should the employee be asked to supply information of this sort in essay form? Probably not, unless the employee usually expresses himself in writing. A supervisor or manager with some preparation on what to ask might question the employee and jot down what is said. Later the comments can be recorded when exit interview information is tabulated.*

Example 3: *Wholesalers L offers the following reasons why it would like to talk with employees upon their departure by telling employees, "At the time of your leaving our employment, we will be glad to review all circumstances of your termination with you. Among the things to be arranged are:*
1. *return of all company property or settlement of any debts owed, prior to the preparation of your final paycheck;*
2. *explanation of the conversion privileges and termination date of your group insurance policies;*
3. *explanation of the provisions under the Unemployment Insurance Regulations in our area; and*
4. *use of the company's name as a future reference.*

Also, we will want your honest opinion of our company practices and policies in order that we may try to improve them."

Alternative to face-to-face interviews. In the event you cannot arrange face-to-face interviews, you may send a questionnaire to an individual's home to be completed and returned. Enclose a stamped self-addressed envelope. Maintain careful records to compare information about those who respond with those who do not.

Who should conduct the exit interview? Here are some key considerations to take into account when selecting an interviewer to conduct exit interviews:

- interviewer must be someone with genuine interest and concern for the employee's welfare;
- ensure that the interviewers are ethnically diverse;
- the interviewer must possess emotional stability and an ability to establish rapport for the give and take necessary to obtaining pertinent information;
- interviewer must have the ability to view people and their situations objectively;
- the interviewer must be knowledgeable about the company's workforce and the company's business; and
- the interviewer should be familiar with the personal history of the employee as well as the work performance record and the employee's working conditions.

An employee leaving a position is an important source of information about the job. You can learn a lot through the exit interview. To aid in this learning process, incorporate these questions into the exit interview.

- Was the job accurately explained to you when you were hired?
- What were the most important parts of your job?
- What were the least important parts of your job?
- How did you spend the majority of your time?
- What skills and training did you have when you were hired?
- What skills and training did you find you needed after you were hired?
- What duties or parts of the job did not seem to fit?
- What other duties are performed in the work unit that could be more logically grouped with the duties of your job?

The Quiz

1. It's ok to immediately fire an employee who has committed a serious offense. ❑ True   ❑ False

2. The WARN Act is a federal law that requires some employers to give 60 days notice of plant closings and mass layoffs. ❑ True   ❑ False

3. Pressuring an employee to resign to avoid being fired could be interpreted as coercion. ❑ True   ❑ False

4. Exit interviews are a good way to collect information that will identify strategies that reduce employee turnover. ❑ True   ❑ False

Answer key: 1. F; 2. T; 3. T; 4. T

Index

Age discrimination
   Benefits ... *65-69*
   Checklist ... *134*
   Employment ads ... *25*
   Generally ... *4, 143-144*
   Harassment ... *154*
   Performance appraisals ... *88*
   Phrases to avoid ... *25-26*
   State laws ... *144, 149*
   Waivers, best practices ... *69*
   Waivers, checklist ... *68*
   Worst case scenario ... *19*
Age Discrimination in Employment Act of 1967 (ADEA)—*see Age discrimination*
Americans with Disabilities Act of 1990 (ADA)
   Accommodation ... *22-23, 126-127, 147*
   FMLA ... *116-118*
   Health insurance ... *72-76*
   Hiring, checklist ... *23*
   Impermissible questions ... *27, 182*
   Leave policies ... *120*
   Medical record ... *36*
   Pre-employment testing ... *31-32*
   Pregnancy ... *122*
   Overlap of leave laws ... *116-128*
   Waivers, best practices ... *69*
   Waivers, checklist ... *68*
Avoidance of legal trouble
   Best practices ... *12*

Benefits
   Equal cost defense checklist ... *66*
Best Practices
   Age claim waivers ... *69*
   Avoidance of legal trouble ... *12*
   Compensation ... *77*
   Discipline ... *191, 217*
   Employee leave, design of ... *111*
   Employment ads ... *25*

   Harassment investigations ... *166-167*
   Hiring decisions ... *21*
   Immigration law requirements ... *40-41*
   Investigations ... *166-167, 217*
   Job descriptions ... *21*
   Leave policies, coordination of ... *120*
   Merit system ... *54*
   Performance appraisals ... *90, 97, 100-101*
   Pre-employment testing ... *31*
   Supervisors, training of ... *203-204*
   Termination ... *217*
   Unfair labor practices, avoidance of ... *203-204*
   Unions, avoidance of ... *208-209*
Bureau of Immigration and Customs Enforcement, Department of Justice ... *7*
Bureau of Labor Statistics, Department of Labor ... *206*

Checklists
   Accommodation of disabilities, reasonable ... *147*
   Age claim waivers ... *68*
   Benefits ... *66*
   Communication, NLRA dos and don'ts ... *204*
   Disabilities, impermissible questions ... *182*
   Documentation ... *183*
   Employment contracts, avoidance of ... *38*
   Essential job functions ... *21*
   Equal cost defense ... *66*
   Equal pay ... *50, 55, 62, 63 - 64*
   Exit interview ... *233*
   FMLA notice ... *109*
   FMLA prohibited employer practices ... *114*
   Gender harassment ... *141*
   Harassment, examples of unlawful conduct ... *157*
   Hiring, ADA compliance ... *23*
   Investigations, choosing investigator ... *167*

Key federal antidiscrimination laws ... *134*
Legality review, terminations ... *219-220*
Medical certification, FMLA ... *112*
Merit-based pay ... *53*
NLRA communication
  dos and don'ts ... *204*
NLRA—concerted or personal activity? ... *198*
Objective/subjective
  performance criteria ... *91*
Performance appraisal meeting ... *99*
Performance appraisal system ... *83*
Promotion denials ... *92*
Reasonable accommodation
  of disabilities ... *147*
Reductions in force ... *223*
Sex discrimination in
  compensation ... *63-64*
Sexual harassment ... *141*
Termination, meeting ... *226*
Termination, questions prior to ... *218-219*
Terminations, exit interview ... *233*
Terminations, legality review ... *219-220*
Terminations, voluntary ... *229*
Training programs ... *57*
Voluntary terminations ... *229*
Citizenship discrimination ... *144*
Civil Rights Act of 1964,
  Title VII
  Checklist ... *134*
  Compensation ... *63*
  Generally ... *3-4*
  Phrases to avoid ... *25-26*
  Pregnancy ... *121*
Color discrimination ... *135-136*
Communication
  Dos and don'ts, checklist ... *204*
Compensation
  Best practices ... *77*
  Equal cost defense ... *66*
  Equal Pay ... *50, 55, 62*
  Equal Pay Act of 1963 (EPA) ... *5, 45-46, 55-57, 63-64, 71, 134*

Merit-based ... *53*
Sex discrimination ... *63-64*
Title VII of Civil Rights Act of 1964 ... *63*
Training programs ... *57*
Consumer credit reports ... *34*

Department of Labor ... *6, 7, 109, 206, 221*
Disabilities
  Accommodation ... *22-23, 147*
  Benefits ... *72-76*
  Best practices ... *120*
  FMLA ... *116*
  Impermissible questions ... *182*
  Interviews ... *27-28*
  Leaves ... *108*
  Pre-employment testing ... *31-32*
  Record checks ... *36*
Discipline
  Best practices ... *191*
  Coaching ... *172, 175-176*
  Communication ... *174, 192*
  Consistency ... *176*
  Counseling ... *179-183*
  Documentation ... *183-193, 217*
  Effective system ... *170-174*
  Investigations ... *177-179*
  Responsibility ... *170*
Discrimination ... *129-151*
  Age—see Age discrimination
  Color discrimination ... *135-136*
  Disability—see Disability discrimination
  Laws prohibiting ... *134-150*
  Intentional ... *130-132*
  Military service ... *148*
  National origin discrimination ... *136-137*
  Pregnancy ... *138-139*
  Race—see Racial discrimination
  Religion—see Religious discrimination
  Sex ... *137-139*
  State laws ... *149-150*
  Unintentional ... *132-133*

Index **239**

Documentation
   Checklist ... *182*
   Discipline, performance
      and termination ... *183-192, 217*
   Harassment ... *167*
   Hiring ... *41*
   How to ... *186-192*
   Immigration ... *6, 39*
   Investigations ... *217*
   Leave ... *126*
   Performance appraisals ... *84-85, 87*
   Supervisor reluctance,
      worst case scenario ... *188*
   Supervisor training ... *186-190*
   Termination ... *87, 218, 222*
Drug and alcohol tests
   ADA issues ... *31*

Employee leave ... *103-128*
   Best practices ... *111, 120*
   Overlap of leave laws ... *116-128*
Employee relations ... *195-213*
   Basic labor rights ... *196-209*
   Employee handbook ... *210-213*
   Unions ... *196-209*
Employment ads
   Best practices ... *25*
Employment contracts, avoidance of
   Checklist ... *38*
English-only rules ... *136-137*
Equal cost defense
   Checklist ... *66*
Equal Employment Opportunity Commission (EEOC)
   ADA ... *75-76*
   Checklist ... *63, 66*
   Equal Pay Act ... *46, 71*
   Guidance ... *24-25*
   Harassment ... *141*
   Settlements ... *69*
Equal pay
   Checklists ... *50, 55, 62*

Equal Pay Act of 1963 (EPA) ... *5, 45-46, 55-57, 63-64, 71, 134*
Essential job functions
   Checklist ... *21*
Exit interview
   Checklist ... *233*

Fair Credit Reporting Act (FCRA) ... *179*
Family and Medical Leave Act (FMLA)
   Bargaining agreements ... *113*
   Best practices ... *111*
   Checklists ... *109, 114*
   Designation of leave ... *110*
   Eligibility for leave ... *107*
   Employers covered ... *106*
   Generally ... *104*
   Leave policies ... *120*
   Medical certification ... *112*
   Notification ... *108-109*
   Overlap of leave laws ... *116-128*
   Paid leaves ... *113*
   Prohibited employer practices
      checklist ... *114*
   Return to work ... *113-114*
   Serious health condition ... *105-106*
Federal antidiscrimination laws
   Checklist of key laws ... *134*

Gender
   Harassment checklist ... *141*
Genetic tests ... *30*

Handbook ... *210*
Harassment ... *153-168*
   Age-based ... *154*
   Complaint, lack of ... *162*
   Coworker ... *159-160*
   Documentation ... *167*
   Forms of ... *155-157*
   Gender, checklist ... *141*
   Grievance procedures ... *165-166*
   Hostile work environment ... *154-155*

Investigation of ... *166-167*
Outsider ... *160-161*
Policies ... *163-165*
Preventive/protective
  measures ... *162-168*
Racial ... *154, 158*
Religious ... *154, 158*
Rude conduct ... *161*
Sexual ... *140-142, 157-158*
Sexual orientation ... *159*
State laws ... *164*
Supervisor ... *142, 155, 159-160, 162-166, 180*
Third party ... *160-161*
Types of ... *157-159*
Unlawful conduct, checklist ... *157*
Harassment investigations
  Best practices ... *166-167*
Hiring ... *15-42*
  Accommodations, reasonable ... *22-23*
  ADA compliance ... *22-23, 36-37*
  Age-based, worst case scenario ... *19*
  Best practices ... *21*
  Credit checks ... *34*
  Criminal records ... *34*
  Documentation ... *41*
  Employment ads ... *25*
  Equal employment
    opportunity compliance ... *17-19*
  Essential job functions ... *20-21*
  Immigration law requirements ... *39-41*
  Interview questions to avoid ... *26-29*
  Job descriptions ... *19-21*
  Job offers ... *37-38*
  Medical records ... *36*
  Recruitment practices ... *24-25*
  References and
    background checks ... *32-33*
Hostile work environment ... *154-155*

Investigations
  Best practices ... *217*
  Choosing investigator, checklist ... *167*
  Questions prior to termination,
    checklist ... *218-219*
Immigration law requirements
  Best practices ... *40-41*
  Documentation ... *6, 39*
  I-9 form ... *40*
  Non-discrimination ... *16*
  Recordkeeping ... *6, 39*
Immigration Reform and
  Control Act (IRCA) ... *6-7, 16, 39-40, 134*
Interracial marriage ... *135*

Job descriptions
  hiring decisions ... *21*

Labor rights ... *196-211*
Lawsuits
  Avoidance of ... *12, 16-19, 211-213*
  Consequences ... *9-11*
Leave ... *103-128*
  Company-offered ... *125-126*
  Coordination of policies ... *120*
  Documentation ... *126*
  Military ... *123-126, 128*
  Overlap of leave laws ... *116-128*
  Pregnancy ... *7, 106, 111, 118, 121-122*
  State laws ... *120*
Legal trouble
  Avoidance of ... *12, 16-19, 211-213*
  Consequences ... *9-11*
Litigation
  Performance appraisals ... *90, 97*

Medical certification
  Checklist ... *112*
Merit system
  Best practices ... *54*
  Equal pay checklist ... *53*
Military service ... *5-6, 16, 28, 37, 123-126, 128, 130, 148, 219, 220*
  Leave ... *123-126, 128*
  Uniformed Services Employment
    and Reemployment Act of 1994
    (USERRA) ... *5, 123-124, 128, 134*

National Labor Relations Act (NLRA)
   Best practices ... *203*
   Checklists ... *198, 204*
   Communication ... *204*
   Concerted activity ... *197-198*
   Election ... *205*
   Generally ... *7-8, 196*
   Interference by employer ... *200*
   Organizing campaigns ... *201*
   Protected activity ... *199*
   Unfair labor practice ... *197, 203*
National Labor Relations Board ... *8*
National origin discrimination ... *136-137*

Office of Federal Contract
   Compliance Programs (OFCCP) ... *7, 77*
Office of Special Counsel,
   Department of Justice ... *7*

Performance appraisals
   Best practices ... *90, 97, 100-101*
   Checklists ... *83, 91, 99*
   Documentation ... *84-85*
   Negative ... *100-101*
   Subjective criteria,
     worst case scenario ... *86-87*
Pre-employment testing ... *29-32*
   Best practices ... *31*
Pregnancy
   Americans with Disabilities Act ... *122*
   Discrimination ... *138-139*
   Discrimination, worst case scenario ... *139*
   Equal pay act ... *71*
   Generally ... *103, 138-139*
   Insurance coverage ... *46, 71-72*
   Leave ... *7, 106, 111, 118, 121-122*
   Title VII of the Civil Rights Act of 164 ... *121*
Pregnancy Discrimination Act of 1978 ... *71*
Promotions
   Checklist, lawful bases for denial ... *92*

Racial discrimination
   Checklist ... *219*
   Compensation ... *65*
   Generally ... *3, 134-135*
   Harassment ... *154, 158*
   Hiring ... *16*
   Insurance ... *70*
   Interviewing ... *26*
   Performance appraisals ... *83, 89*
   Protected groups ... *130*
   Unintentional discrimination ... *132*
Reductions in force
   Checklist ... *223*
Religious accommodation ... *185*
Religious discrimination
   Benefits ... *65, 76*
   Checklist ... *219*
   Generally ... *3, 143*
   Harassment ... *154, 158*
   Interviewing ... *26, 28*
Religious harassment ... *154, 158*
Reverse discrimination ... *142*
Rude conduct ... *161*

Sex discrimination ... *137-139*
   Compensation ... *63-64*
   Pregnancy ... *138-139*
Sexual harassment ... *140-142, 157-158*
Sexual orientation ... *8, 16, 142, 149-150, 159, 219*
State laws
   Age discrimination ... *144, 149*
   Consumer credit reports ... *34*
   Criminal records ... *34-36*
   Disabilities ... *72-76*
   Discrimination ... *149-150*
   Employee leave ... *120-121, 125*
   Insurance ... *72-76*
   Medical insurance ... *72*
   Overlap of leave laws ... *116-128*
   Performance appraisals ... *83*
   Privacy ... *34*
   Sexual harassment ... *164*
   Sexual orientation ... *8, 16, 142, 149-150, 159*
   Source of employee rights ... *8-9, 16, 26-27*

Veterans ... *148*
 Workers' compensation ... *119-120*
Supervisors
 Coaching ... *172, 175-176*
 Discipline ... *170-174, 176, 182*
 Documentation, worst case scenario ... *188*
 Harassment ... *142, 155, 159-160, 162-166, 180*
 Labor relations ... *197, 199, 203-205, 208*
 Statements attributable to organization ... *78*
 Termination authority ... *230-231*
 Training ... *12-13, 54, 83, 92-98, 104, 126, 162-166, 174, 178-179, 186-190, 203-205, 208, 216, 224, 231*
Suspensions
 During investigation ... *216*
 Union activity ... *216*

Termination
 Best practices ... *217*
 Documentation ... *87, 217-218, 222*
 Exit interviews ... *231-235*
 Exit interview, checklist ... *233*
 Groups of employees ... *220-221*
 How to ... *217- 228*
 Investigation, best practices ... *217*
 Investigation, checklist ... *218-219*
 Legality review, checklist ... *219-220*
 Meeting, checklist ... *226*
 Meeting, conducting ... *223-228*
 Notice ... *221-223*
 Prompted ... *229-231*
 Reductions in force, checklist ... *223*
 Supervisor authority ... *230-231*
 Voluntary ... *228-229*
 Voluntary, checklist ... *229*
 Worker Adjustment and Retraining Notification Act ... *221-223*
Testing, pre-employment ... *31*
 Best practices
Time away from work

 Company-offered ... *125-126*
 Coordination of policies ... *120*
 Military ... *123-125*
 Pregnancy ... *121-122*
 State laws ... *120*
Title VII of the Civil Rights Act of 1964 — *see Civil Rights Act of 1964*
Training programs
 Compensation ... *57*

Unfair labor practices
 Avoidance of ... *203-204*
 Supervisor training ... *203-204*
Uniformed Services Employment and Reemployment Rights Act of 1994 (USERRA) ... *5-6, 123-124, 128, 134*
Unions
 Best practices ... *208-209*
 Elections ... *205*
 Membership ... *206*
 Organizing campaign ... *201*

Veterans ... *6, 28, 148, 154, 219*
Veterans Employment and Training Service, Department of Labor (VETS) ... *6*

Wage and Hour Division, Department of Labor ... *109*
Waivers, age claims
 Best practices ... *69*
Worker Adjustment and Retraining Notification Act ... *221-223*
Workers' Compensation
 Leave policies ... *120*
 Overlap of leave laws ... *116-128*
Worst case scenario
 Age-based hiring decision ... *19*
 Documentation, supervisor reluctance ... *188*
 Pregnancy discrimination ... *139*
 Subjective performance criteria ... *86-87*